TEACHING JEWISHLY

Joel Lurie Grishaver

TORAH AURA PRODUCTIONS

ISBN 10: 1-891662-06-1
ISBN 13: 978-1-891662-06-8

Torah Aura Productions • 4423 Fruitland Avenue, Los Angeles, CA 90058 (800) BE-Torah • (800) 238-6724 • (323) 585-7312 • fax (323) 585-0327 E-MAIL <misrad@torahaura.com> • Visit the Torah Aura website at www. torahaura.com

MANUFACTURED IN UNITED STATES OF AMERICA

For Jim Fay

For Rabbi Zelig Pliskin

This book is a fantasy.

It started with what would happen if Jim Fay (a noted secular teacher educator) and Rabbi Zelig Pliskin (a master of Jewish sources) met and had a conversation about teaching.

Table of Contents

TEACHING JEWISHLY

This book is based on a very simple idea.

I always used to think that what I taught was Jewish and that the way I taught reflected the best of Western teaching technology. In my mind, my classroom was Jewish as long as I was productively transferring Jewish values. When I had to deal with a classroom problem I stopped my Jewish teaching and went into a defensive posture. This was classroom management mode, and to get into that, I dropped out of Jewish teaching mode. When the problem was solved, I went back to Jewish teaching.

Eventually I figured out that this was a mistake. I began to realize that some of the most important Jewish teaching and modeling I did happened when I dealt with classroom management issues.

Here are a few things we know are true:

- When we deal with students who are acting badly we have our most important chance to teach about Jewish values.

- Instead of thinking of behavioral incidents as interruptions of our Jewish teaching, is possible to think of these moments as important Jewish teaching opportunities.

- A surprising number of Jewish teachers were once "problem children"; when we deal well with our difficult students we are building the future of Jewish education.

- The Jewish tradition actually offers tools and insights that make it easier for teachers to deal with their students.

Talmudic Truth

The "teaching wisdom" in this book did not start in my own experience, nor did it come from deep psychological studies, though it has been enriched by both of those. The truths here come from the Talmud and other Jewish sources that grew from it. It is "Rabbinic wisdom."

"The Rabbis" (the Talmudic Rabbis) were a group of scholars who reinvented Judaism between 200 B.C.E. and 500 C.E. They took the state-religion of a nation that was based on a priesthood, a Temple, and big pageants and turned it into a religion that used rituals and practices done in home and community. They took the Bible and its general values and turned them into day-to-day things that helped people to make them real in their lives.

The Rabbis believed that God's vision for people included three goals: (1) that people should come to be close to God, (2) that each person should become the best person he or she can be, and (3) that together people should make the world into the best possible place for all people. In the Torah the rabbis found 613 *mitzvot*. These were things that God told us to either make sure we do or make sure we don't do. Some of these *mitzvot* directly affect the way we treat other people, while others were designed as "training exercises," ways of getting us into condition to do the other ????. It is not always clear which is which.

This book is not designed to be a "religious" book in the sense that it will talk about keeping kosher or praying every day. It was written by culling parts of the tradition that specifically and directly deal with the ways that we (a) take care of ourselves, (b) treat others, and (c) get ourselves in condition to do the other two. It will be a religious book in the sense that if it does impact the relationship between you and your students, if it does help you to be more aware of the good you can do and to act in ways you believe are right, those accomplishments are religious. It also might lead you to connect to the tradition in other ways—but it is not directly designed to do that.

Nachman of Bretzlav was a Hasidic master who lived about the same time as Abraham Lincoln. He taught:

All people reach in three directions. They reach in to find themselves. They reach out to find others. And they reach up to find God. The miracle in the way that God created the universe is that when we grasp in any one of these directions we wind up making contact in all three.

While this book is only concerned with relationships between people, it has the possibility of making all kinds of connections.

Jewish Values

This is a book about taking Jewish values and wisdom learned from Jewish texts and turning them into a process of teaching, a Jewish way of teaching. It is the direct application of Jewish values and Jewish process to the task of running a classroom. The idea to make this connection is almost obvious and grows out of numerous Jewish literatures. First, starting with the Talmud and moving on through *Mussar* (ethical) texts, there are numerous discussions of the way that a teacher should treat students. The Rabbis of the Talmud all thought of themselves as teachers, so the "art of teaching" was a big topic of concern for them. Second, much of Jewish literature focuses on how to act well in stressful situations. In many ways, acting well in stressful situations is the epitome of the task of the teacher who is trying to exercise control in difficult classroom situations. Discussions of controlling anger, giving negative feedback, and helping people change their behavior are all big issues for the Rabbis and simultaneously real concerns for teachers.

But this material has not been created in an exclusively Jewish context. All of it has been measured against and compared to numerous selections from secular classroom management literature. Often the conjunctions and confluences are wonderful. Many times Jewish sources helped to deepen and focus recommended practices. Most importantly, they often add a spiritual dimension, helping us to turn mundane problems into holy moments.

TEACHERS ARE SUPPOSED TO BE ANGELS

Hevruta Study

You need to rethink most of what you know about angels. No wings. No halo. No white choir robes. And forget the bit about angels being dead people walking around on clouds.

For Jews the Hebrew word for angel is *malakh* (messenger). *Malakhim* can be human or part of the divine realm.

> The main contribution of Hasidic thought to angelology was a distinctly anthropocentric, even psychological, interpretation of angelic nature. Specifically, early Hasidic masters held that ephemeral angels were the direct result of human action. Goodly deeds created good angels, destructive behavior created destructive angels, etc.
>
> Encyclopedia Mythica, "Angels" by Rabbi Geoffrey W. Dennis
> http://www.pantheon.org/articles/a/angels.html

> An angel is a packet of divine energy.
>
> The Zohar

> Angels are the creation of our own positive thoughts, words, and deeds.
>
> Midrash Tanhuma

> The angels mediate between God and man. They carry the prayers up to the throne of God (Tobit, 12.12). According to Exodus Rabbah 21, an angel set over the prayers weaves them into crowns for the Most High. Angels intercede for

those who dwell on earth (Enoch, 60), which is to be translated: "If there be on a person's side one, this is like a single messenger among a thousand pleading for him"). They pray for Adam's pardon (Apoc. Mosis, 33) and offer praise to God after the same has been granted (*Ibid., 37*).

Jewish Encyclopedia

Rabbi Morris Margolies, who wrote *A Gathering of Angels*, teaches that angels are best understood as symbols of forces that operate within us, metaphors for the most basic human drives and emotions: love, hate, envy, lust, charity, malice, greed, generosity, vision, despair, fear, hope. God doesn't need angels, but mortals do. Angels narrow the chasm that separates us from God: The angels are near God, but not part of God.

http://www.scheinerman.net/judaism/ideas/angels.html

MAY THE ANGEL WHO HAS REDEEMED ME FROM ALL HARM BLESS THESE CHILDREN.

Jacob's blessing to his grandsons Ephraim and Menashe (Genesis 48:16)

AND JACOB SAID TO JOSEPH: "GO AND SEE WHETHER IT IS WELL WITH YOUR BROTHERS, AND WELL WITH THE FLOCK; AND BRING BACK WORD TO ME." SO HE SENT HIM OUT OF THE VALLEY OF HEBRON, AND HE CAME TO SHECHEM. AND A CERTAIN MAN FOUND HIM WHEN HE WAS WANDERING IN THE FIELD. AND THE MAN ASKED HIM, SAYING: "WHAT ARE YOU SEEKING?" AND HE SAID: "I SEEK MY BROTHERS. PLEASE TELL ME WHERE THEY ARE FEEDING THE FLOCK." AND THE MAN SAID: "THEY LEFT HERE; FOR I HEARD THEM SAY: 'LET US GO TO DOTHAN.'" AND JOSEPH WENT AFTER HIS BROTHERS AND FOUND THEM IN DOTHAN.

Genesis 37.14-17

The angel who met Joseph in the field was not winged or terrifying; he was just a messenger angel—a man who was also an angel from God. Joseph surely did not know that this man was an angel, and the man himself may not even have known, yet he was a *malakh*, a messenger bearing a message from God that was both important and fragile. Important because it was a message from God and hearing it changed Joseph's life, but fragile because Joseph might not have heard it. He could easily have dismissed the stranger's directions to Dothan, figuring that he might have confused his brothers with some other shepherds heading that way. Angels present us with a message but also a choice—the choice of whether or not we can hear the message.

Marc Gellman, http://www.leaderu.com/ftissues/ft9703/articles/gellman.html

Teachers are expected to reach *unattainable* goals with *inadequate* tools. The miracle is that at times they accomplish this impossible task.

Haim Ginott, *Teachers: A Tribute*

Being an Angel

Listen to this piece of Talmud:

> Rabbah bar Bar Hana said that Rabbi Yohanan said: "What is the meaning of Malachi 2.7: 'FOR THE PRIEST'S LIPS SHOULD KEEP KNOWLEDGE, AND THEY SHOULD SEEK THE LAW AT HIS MOUTH; FOR HE IS THE MESSENGER OF THE ETERNAL-OF-HOSTS"? This means that if the teacher is like an angel, they should seek Torah at the teacher's mouth...
>
> *Haggigah* 15b

The Talmud teaches that a teacher must resemble an angel. We know a lot of things about angels:

- Angels are messengers of God.
- Angels "serve and protect."
- Angels have the job of praising God.
- Angels are a way for people to wrestle with God.
- Angels go up and down (from heaven to earth).

These are all pretty good attributes for teachers. The bottom line is that Jewish teachers represent God in their classrooms; they speak for God. Just as God deals with difficult individuals who have free will, so does the teacher. Just as God often has to try again and give second chances, so do teachers. And remember this: No matter how difficult, no matter the struggle, teachers are not in the classroom to teach their own message; they are there to bring Torah—God's word.

Blue Ink

I know two things about this story. First, it comes from a book called *Bastions of Faith*, which I no longer remember. Second, I know that when I use it in workshops some teachers misunderstand it. Still, it is powerful enough to use here. (And I know you will get it—that is positive reinforcement!)

Rabbi Moshe Feinstein, one of the greatest Jewish legal authorities in the world, used to teach a high school Talmud class once a week. He used to use his grandfather's edition of the Talmud for this class. Once he got called out of the class for a phone call, and while he was away the students (for reasons known only to students) began to toss a bottle of ink around the room. Somehow the bottle fell on the open Talmud and spilled down the page. With the students in shock, Rabbi Feinstein returned to the room. He looked at the page, then at the students, then back at the page. Once again his eyes rose to the class, a smile came to his face, he held the book up to the class, and he said, "Doesn't this page look good in blue?"

When I tell this story to teachers, some of them get angry that he failed to chastise his students. They don't understand that these students, elite seniors who were studying with one of the leading Talmud scholars in the world, had already been chastised by their own actions. Other teachers were angry that he didn't make them responsible for their actions. They don't get that the book was priceless, and no action could repair or replace it. What they miss is the act of forgiveness, the commitment to not shame, and the powerful model of controlling anger that Rabbi Feinstein manifested.

I don't know what the rest of the conversation in the classroom was. That is not part of the story I read. I don't know if he allowed or invited acts of *tzedakah* or anything else. What I do know is that Rabbi Feinstein was being an angel—modeling God in his actions.

Before we go any further, it is important to remember that our students' Jewish identity and their relationship to God will both be heavily influenced by the teacher's relationship with the students. All this is about being a messenger, a *malakh*, an angel.

In a lesson that we will come to in the next chapter, the Rav, Rabbi Joseph Soloveitchik, taught: "I like being around students, and I become one of the gang. That is the only way to teach. A teacher who does not lose years in the classroom and does not become one of his class cannot teach Torah successfully. You teach pals and friends. You do not teach anything to anyone who is below you! This is my philosophy of teaching Torah!"

Being an angel is both a metaphor and a reality. Angels are messengers of God; they need not be celestial creatures. Our job is to convey God's message.

TEACHING AS RELATIONSHIP

Hevruta Study

JUST AS FACE ANSWERS FACE IN A REFLECTION IN WATER,
SO SHOULD ONE PERSON'S HEART ANSWER ANOTHER.

Proverbs 27.19

All real living is meeting.

Martin Buber

My reading of Buber has changed me as a person and a teacher. His concept of dialogue or "I–Thou" relationship has singularly affected me when I listen to students, conceive of who they are in my classroom, and interact with them in office hours. The I–Thou simply means that we are constantly in dialogue with the world, and as such, every part of the world (people, animals, even inanimate objects!) needs to be treated as an equal, a subject (rather than an object) of our discussion and thoughts. The I–Thou is the source of all positive interaction in the world.

Richard Freund, University of Hartford, CT
http://www.aarweb.org/Publications/spotlight/previous/7-2/07-02.asp

A teacher once came to the Hazon Ish and asked his advice about changing professions. S/he wanted to become a diamond polisher. "Aren't you already a diamond polisher?" asked the Hazon Ish.

Biography of Hazon Ish, p. 229

"HOLY IS THE ETERNAL OF HOSTS, THE WHOLE EARTH IS FULL OF GOD'S GLORY" (Isaiah 6.3). The angels are all joined to one another, and dovetail into one another, just as the boards of the Tabernacle were "INTER-LOCKED ONE TO ONE OTHER" (Exodus 26.17). The boards stood ever upright and did not bend, just as the angels, the "standing ones", who, having no joints, never bend. As the boards had two holders which united one board with the next, so is one angel joined to the other: each one takes his own and his neighbor's wing, and so enfolded within each other they stand closely united. Of the Torah the same is true: the students both teach and learn from one another in perfect reciprocity

Zohar, Shemot, Section 2, Page 171a

Imagine someone had a child living in a distant city; would that parent not wish to find a person of integrity to teach the child wisdom and proper behavior? This is exactly what one should be willing to do for one's students. This idea is covered by the mitzvah of "LOVING YOUR NEIGHBOR AS YOURSELF" (Leviticus 19.18).

Ahavat Hesed, Part 3, Chapter 7, *Chofetz Chayim*

I am a survivor of a concentration camp. My eyes saw what no person should witness. Gas chambers built by learned engineers. Children poisoned by educated physicians. Infants killed by trained nurses. Women and babies shot and killed by high school and college graduates. So I'm suspicious of education. My request is: help your students to be human. Your efforts must never produce learned monsters, skilled psychopaths, or educated Eichmanns. Reading and writing and spelling and history and arithmetic are only important if they serve to make our students more human.

Haim Ginott

What is the mitzvah of Jewish teaching?

The first guess is almost always וְשִׁנַּנְתָּם לְבָנֶיךָ *v-shi'nantam l'vanekha*, "AND YOU SHALL TEACH THEM DILIGENTLY TO YOUR CHILDREN" (Deuteronomy 6.7). But there is a problem with this verse. It is understood to be the verse that obligates parents to educate their children; it doesn't obligate an outside teacher. The Jewish tradition solves this problem two different ways.

Way One: Make Your Students into Relatives

Maimonides teaches:

> Just as parents are obligated to teach Torah to their children so too they are obligated to teach their grandchildren. We learn this from Deuteronomy 4.9, "AND YOU SHALL MAKE THEM (the words of Torah) KNOWN TO YOUR CHILDREN AND GRANDCHILDREN." And this is not only to your child and grandchild, but it is a mitzvah for teachers to teach any student.
>
> Maimonides, *Laws of Talmud Torah* 1.2

In a midrashic collection we are taught that it is a responsibility for teachers to "adopt" the children of others when they teach them. This goes back to when Joshua ben Gamla appointed community teachers to supplement what parents could do—especially for students without parents.

Sifrei, Deuteronomy 6.7

Rambam uses the mitzvah of וְשִׁנַּנְתָּם לְבָנֶיךָ *v-shi'nantam l'vanekha,* "AND YOU SHALL TEACH THEM DILIGENTLY TO YOUR CHILDREN" (Deuteronomy 6.7), as the source for teachers to teach students. The only way that this can make sense is if וְשִׁנַּנְתָּם *v-shi'nantam* means to treat the student as your own child. You cannot teach a student until you adopt

them. Making the student "as your own child" is part of
the mitzvah of וְשִׁנַּנְתָּם v-shi'nantam (you shall teach them).

Rabbi Noach Orlowek, My Disciple, My Child

Rabbi Zelig Pliskin, Love Your Neighbor, retells a story that makes
this clear. Rabbi Yisrael Yaakov Lubchanski worked on changing
a student's attitude for months. He got nowhere and eventually
gave up. He began to treat the student as a ghost, someone who
was basically not there. After a time the rabbi, who was childless,
began to wonder, "What if this difficult boy was my own son?
Why do I give up on him just because he belongs to someone
else?" This reflection changed Rabbi Lubchanski's attitude toward
the boy and that changed the nature of their relationship. The
rabbi began over again. Eventually the once-difficult boy grew up
to be an outstanding leader.

Adapted secondhand from an article by Rabbi Chayim Shaprio
Jewish Observer, January 1971

The Other Way: Love Your Neighbor

Originally Jewish teachers (including scholars) taught for free. The
idea was that God gave them the Torah (for free), and they should
give Torah for free (just like God). They considered getting paid
for teaching Torah like turning the Torah into a spade. This worked
for a while, but then teachers couldn't afford to be teachers, and
the quality of education dropped. The Rabbis responded with a
legal fiction. They allowed teachers to be paid for the time they
gave, not for the Torah they shared. They used the analogy of a
babysitter. Torah teachers were paid for babysitting.

At first this may sound denigrating, but then I want to tell you
about Betty Mahoney. I am sure you had one of your own.
When I was young, Betty Mahoney was my babysitter. She once
knitted me a pair of red wool mittens with a string that connected
the mittens and ran through the sleeves of a jacket. It was with
her that I first (helped) make chocolate pudding and had lots of

other adventures. Betty was the first adult (high school kid) with whom I ever spent significant time other than my parents. She was almost part of the family for a while, and it was clear that I "loved" her and she "loved" me. Our relationship was a lot more than contractual.

The Chofetz Chayim used this understanding when he taught:

> Imagine someone had a child living in a distant city; would that parent not wish to find a person of integrity to teach the child wisdom and proper behavior? This is exactly what one should be willing to do for one's students. This idea is covered by the mitzvah of "LOVING YOUR NEIGHBOR AS YOURSELF" (Leviticus 19.18).
>
> *Ahavat Hesed, Part 3, Chapter 7, Chofetz Chayim*

The Chofetz Chayim is saying that וְשִׁנַּנְתָּם לְבָנֶיךָ *v-shi'nantam l'vanekha*, "AND YOU SHALL TEACH THEM DILIGENTLY TO YOUR CHILDREN" (Deuteronomy 6.7), is indeed a parent's mitzvah. Jewish teaching comes out of a different verse: וְאָהַבְתָּ לְרֵעֲךָ כָּמוֹךָ *v'ahavta l'rayakha k'mokha*, "LOVE YOUR NEIGHBOR AS YOURSELF" (Leviticus 19.18). Torah teaching is an act of love.

The bottom line here is that the Chofetz Chayim teaches that Jewish teaching is an act of love, and love is a dynamic relationship.

Classroom Community

While we will focus on the classroom as a learning community later in this text, it is important to underline the fact that the relationship between learners is as important as the relationship between student and teacher. Traditionally Jewish learners worked in *hevrutot* (friendship pairs), from the Hebrew word חָבֵר *haver* (friendship). *Avot d' Rabbi Natan* (an extended version of *Pirkei Avot*) describes one's relationship with one's classmates this way:

A friend is someone you eat and drink with.
A friend is someone with whom you study Torah (God's word)
and with whom you study Mishnah (ethics and laws).
A friend is someone who sleeps over
or at whose house you can spend the night.
Friends teach each other secrets,
the secrets of the Torah
and secrets of the real world, too.

Avot d'Rabbi Natan

The simple lessons of this chapter are that Torah both builds relationships and takes relationships. Being a teacher is an act of love (family or neighborly), and it comes with the responsibility to create friendships among your students.

CLASSROOM MANAGEMENT BEGINS WITH GREETING

Hevruta Study

THE BASIC MITZVAH

Shammai says: "Make of your Torah study a fixed practice; say little and do much;
and greet all people with a cheerful countenance."

Pirkei Avot 1.15

AND GREET ALL PEOPLE WITH A CHEERFUL COUNTENANCE

This teaches that if one person gave another all the good gifts in the world with a downcast face, Torah credits it as though that person had given nothing. But if one greets another with a cheerful countenance, even though that person gives the other nothing, Torah credits it as though the greeter had given the other all the good gifts in the world.

Avot d'Rabbi Natan

WHY GREET PEOPLE WITH A CHEERFUL COUNTENANCE?

[a] Let a person show a happy face to others so that they will be pleased with her.

Rabbi Yonah

[b] Even if your heart does not rejoice when another arrives, pretend to be cheerful; let the other think that your face lights up with joy at his coming.

Meiri

[c] Shammai is here urging three things that are interconnected. They are about three human areas… wisdom, strength, riches… Shammai tells us greet people with a cheerful countenance because it helps you to be strong by mastering anger. We are taught "Who is mighty? One who subdues his/her evil impulse."…A cheerful countenance is the opposite of arrogance and anger.

Shimon ben Zemah Duran

WHY GREETING WORKS

In his commentary to *Shir Ha-Shirim* (Song of Songs) the Vilna Gaon, also known as the Gra, mentions the four major reasons why we wish to be connected with something. They are:

1. *Tov*—**Something good.** We are attracted to things we recognize as having intrinsic goodness.

2. *Areiv*—**sweet.** The prospect of physical pleasure serves as an attraction.

3. *Mo'il*—**utility.** Something we perceive as helpful in achieving our goals will also merit our attention.

   The Gra uses food to illustrate this point. Food can be merely tasty (*areiv*) or nutritious (*mo'il*), or it can be a mitzvah (*tov*), such as a Temple sacrifice or matzah on Pesah.

4. The Gra points out a fourth type of bond: We are drawn to people who care about us. "JUST AS FACE ANSWERS FACE IN A REFLECTION IN WATER, SO SHOULD ONE PERSON'S HEART ANSWER ANOTHER" (Proberbs 27:19).

These four elements also affect teacher–student rapport.
Students respect a teacher who is a proper role model.
Sensing his/her intrinsic goodness (*tov*), they wish to
emulate their teacher.

Rav Moshe Feinstein, *Dorash Moshe*, beginning of *Parashat Toldot*

YOU CAN'T MAKE SOMEONE MAD AND SELL THEM SOMETHING AT THE SAME TIME

1. A person will perform for a person he loves. If he has
   high self-concept and self-love he will do it for himself.
   If high self-concept is not yet developed, that person
   will have to do it for someone else until he learns to love
   himself.

2. It takes years to change self-concept. Even if you use
   highly scientific methods, the change will not show
   up in less than one month per year of the person's age.
   In other words, it will take at least twelve months to
   change the self-concept of a twelve-year-old.

3. In order to change a person's self-concept, the teacher
   must first get that person to take a risk, try to do
   something she believes too difficult.

4. A student will probably only take that risk when he loves
   and trusts the teacher.

From *Teaching with Love and Logic* by Jim Fay and David Funk

TALMUDIC EXAMPLE

It is said that Rabban Yohanan ben Zakkai never ever…let
anyone else open the door to his students. After him, his
disciple Rabbi Eliezer conducted himself in the same way.

Sukkah 28a and *Ein Yaakov*, ad loc.

A Good Offense

To use a sports metaphor, classroom management takes both offense and defense. Defense is when we are forced by a situation to create a response. Offense is the atmosphere and framework we set up in class to encourage participation and to set limits. Classical teacher wisdom states, "A teacher should start strict and then loosen up as the year goes on." Jewish wisdom will teach "Start cheerfully."

A Case Study

This letter came to us via e-mail from a teacher who taught in a one-room schoolhouse with fourth to seventh graders in the same class.

> The class was looking and acting tired, so I had everyone pretend to go to sleep and then say the *Shema*, provided they wake up and sing *Modeh Ani* to get them moving. They were mostly excited and into it, but a few kids basically didn't get up when the "alarm" rang. So 75% of the class was singing *Modeh Ani*, and the others were lying on the floor being difficult. The whole class was looking at me to see what I'd do about it. My instinct was to be hurt and angry that they had taken advantage of my flexibility in lesson planning, but then I tried to smile and ask someone to tap them gently. Eventually they got up, but I ended up feeling embarrassed, like I had lost face.

I often bring this case into workshops and ask people to suggest what this first-year teacher should do. The single most popular answer is "chocolate." Many teachers are into bribing the students who respond positively. The next most popular answers all have to do with other (non-food) modalities of positive reinforcement for the students who are behaving. When I got the letter I asked just one question: "Were the problems the twelve-year-old boys?" I got back a diatribe on all the things these boys and their families do to make this particular teacher's life uncomfortable. I sent the diagnosis that I will share with you now. "Greet all students at the door as they come in every day." This may seem overly simple, but I will explain. The problem here is a relationship problem. Until she fixes the relationship issue with this group of students, one incident after another will occur. But to explain how saying hello fixes things, let's start with some Jewish thinking.

In *Pirkei Avot* 1.15 Shammai says:

> "Make of your Torah study a fixed practice; say little and do much; and greet all people with a cheerful countenance."

We care about the "cheerful countenance" part.

In *Avot d'Rabbi Natan*, a commentary on *Pirkei Avot,* we are taught:

> This teaches that if one person gave another all the good gifts in the world with a downcast face, Torah credits it as though that person had given nothing. But if one greets another with a cheerful countenance, even though that person gives the other nothing, Torah credits it as though the greeter had given the other all the good gifts in the world.

I once abused this insight while trying to teach it. I was giving a 200-teacher workshop, and there were two who were constantly talking. I told everyone quietly over the wireless mike that I was going to demonstrate how this works. I then walked over to these teachers and screamed at them, "I think you are wonderful." The words were a compliment, but the tone was one of anger. The two stood up and yelled back at me. They told me I had no right to speak to them like that. I asked if they had heard what I said.

They responded, "No one has the right to speak to a student in that tone of voice." I had made my point but lost the war; the two of them started to walk out. I spent the next twenty minutes apologizing to them while teaching the importance of teachers apologizing when they are wrong.

Here is the simple truth. Students read our tones. Students read our emotions. And that is the content they drink. Until this teacher can like some aspect of these kids, until they know that, she will have a hard time getting them to respond in any positive ways.

The tradition teaches these three responses to the question "Why greet people with a cheerful countenance?"

> [a] Let a person show a happy face to others so that they will be pleased with her.
>
> Rabbi Yonah

> [b] Even if your heart does not rejoice when another arrives, pretend to be cheerful; let the other think that your face lights up with joy at his coming.
>
> Meiri

> [c] Shammai is here urging three things that are interconnected. They are about three human areas… wisdom, strength, riches… He tells us to greet people with a cheerful countenance because it helps you to be strong by mastering anger. We are taught, "Who is mighty? One who subdues his/her evil impulse."…A cheerful countenance is the opposite of arrogance and anger.
>
> *Shimon ben Zemah Duran*

This last insight by Rabbi Shimon ben Zemah Duran is the reason that classroom management begins at the classroom door. As each student arrives the teacher needs to think of something he or she likes or respects about each one. They then smile and greet in a sincere way. Classroom management begins by reminding us and our students that we like them. That is the beginning of a great offense.

In the book of Ruth we find this verse:

> "AND, BEHOLD, BOAZ CAME FROM BETHLEHEM, AND SAID TO THE REAPERS: 'GOD BE WITH YOU.' AND THEY ANSWERED HIM: 'GOD BLESS YOU.'"

Ruth 2.4

Based on this verse, the Rabbis said it is a mitzvah to be like Boaz and greet every person cheerfully (*Brakhot* 54a). Jews have lots of greetings; different occasions have different greetings. The idea here is that every greeting is acknowledging the spark of God that is in every person.

This Talmudic story manifests this value.

> It is said that Rabban Yoḥanan ben Zakkai never ever…let anyone else open the door to his students. After him, his disciple Rabbi Eliezer conducted himself in the same way.

Sukkah 28a and *Ein Yaakov*, ad loc.

Jim Fay tells a story that starts where the Rabban Yoḥanan ben Zakkai story starts but takes the insight much deeper. He tells of a woman who teaches English in an inner-city school. She has the remedial kids, the worst in the school. And for some reason her car is safe on the street while the other teachers' cars are vandalized in the guarded school parking lot. Once, when a principal's staff meeting threatened to make her late to greet her students at the door, she told him, "Either I meet my students at the door or someone else can teach my class today." The rest of the faculty insisted that she should leave the meeting and greet her class. The teacher explained, "I have to ask my students to do the most difficult thing they will ever have to do. Knives and guns don't scare them. They are part of their lives. But I have to ask them to read out loud or put things down on paper. This is something they are afraid of failing at. I can't ask them do it for

29

you. Because they don't believe they can do it. I have to say, 'Do it for me.' And for them to try, they need to love me. That love begins every morning at the classroom door."

We who teach in Jewish schools, especially part-time Jewish schools, need that same kind of love. And for us it also needs to be built starting at the classroom door. That is how we need to begin with scared preschoolers and how we have to heal our relationships with difficult seventh graders. Greeting is an important part of our school and synagogue cultures. Just listen to this story from the yeshiva world.

> At Rabbi Simha Zissel Ziv's yeshiva in Kelm, students conscientiously worked on the trait of being friendly to strangers. Rabbi Moshe Rosenstein, who later became the *menaheil ruhani* (spiritual mentor) of Lomzhe Yeshiva, often recalled his first day as a young student in Kelm. As soon as he entered the yeshiva building, someone greeted him with a wide smile and inquired about his trip and welfare. The fellow was so friendly that the young Rabbi Rosenstein was certain that he must be an old acquaintance whom he couldn't recall. The same happened with the second and third students he met, until he realized that in Kelm this was the usual reception accorded to strangers.
>
> Zelig Pliskin, *Love Your Neighbor*

My friend Ron Wolfson has written a book called *The Spirituality of Welcoming* that takes the idea of greeting and grows it into an institutional value. It is a wonderful book full of helpful hints. Here is one example. It is Ron's *Art of Dealing with Difficult People*. It is based on the acronym LAST:

L—Listen: The most important thing to do when someone is upset is to listen to his or her story without interruption or any attempt to explain. Just listen.

A—Acknowledge: Say "I'm sorry." It does not matter whether the institution was wrong or the person is out of line. It costs absolutely nothing to express your concern.

S—Solve: As quickly as possible, solve the problem. If you can't solve the problem, connect the person with someone who can.

T—Thank: Thank the individual for bringing the issue to your attention. Assure the person that steps will be taken to improve service. If it becomes clear that the synagogue was at fault, consider creating a memorable recovery by giving something unexpected to the member: a discount, an *aliyah,* a mention in the bulletin.

Ron Wolfson, Spirituality of Welcoming

Ron's list was created for "greeters" in a synagogue. How would you adapt this list for teachers dealing with difficult students and parents?

When I published the original version of this chapter in the *Torah Aura Bulletin Board,* I received this e-mail. It is the best testimonial for this material.

Thank you for your piece on putting on a good face. When my son, who is now twenty-one, was in Hebrew school, he had a problem with a particular teacher. My son is ADHD and oppositional/defiant, so if he knew you didn't like him, he shut down. The teacher complained about him, and I told her she should just fake it—have a one-to-one talk and say how much she liked and cared about him, and that it would help in getting him to do the work. She said she couldn't...I also teach in this school. I had her three children, who were not easy either, and I made sure to be positive with them...What a lesson this woman taught us all! Fortunately, she is no longer teaching in our school. Coincidentally, I also gave the same advice to his Spanish teacher in public school, and he took my advice. Just that small act of kindness made a big difference in their relationship.

Money in the Bank

Money in the Bank is an abstract metaphor for a reality we all know. Think: "I owe you one." Sometimes we can get away with a request that would never be honored for anyone else. Why? Because the other person "owes" us. What they "owe" us is an abstraction. Perhaps we have done a favor, and the "currency" is actually being repaid. More often, we are trading on a connection, a sense of caring, knowing, and understanding.

One secret of working with students, working with adults, and especially working with families is that it is good to have "money in the bank." The rest of the secret is that showing we care is usually the best way to make a deposit.

My friend and teacher Seymour Rossel began his book *Managing the Jewish Classroom* with a chapter called "Remaining Relevant". He started by stating:

> Capturing the student's attention is essential. Even the work of motivation cannot begin if the student and the teacher are not on the same wavelength. And the transformation of teaching into learning depends on teachers, students, and parents working cooperatively. This chapter contains a series of simple and tested activities [techniques] which help teachers, students, and parents interact in useful ways.

Seymour then goes on to suggest a number of strategies that allow the teacher to gather information about student (and parent) interests, starting with an index card that they fill out with a favorite book, movie, album, hobby, TV show, etc. Part of the technique is not in the data collected, but the caring demonstrated by the act of collection. Seymour is very "behaviorist" as a teacher and a teacher trainer. Even though I am more humanist in my orientation, I use all of his techniques. They put "money in the bank."

I often tell the story of my friend Joyce Seglin, who is a truly great school principal. When she was the principal of Temple Emanuel in Beverly Hills she used to stand on the steps every day and say hello and good-bye to every student (and parent) who came or went (before or after school). Every before-school meeting ended in time for Joyce to stand on the steps. Every after-school meeting started after step patrol. These hellos were more than "What's up?" and a nod. Once I saw a little eleven-year-old student mope up the stairs—his eyes were on his shoes—and he looked on the edge of tears. Joyce asked him "How are you doing?" And he said, "My mother kicked my father out of the house again." Joyce looked at him with a great big smile and said, "And things are much better now, right?" The kid's head lifted, and with a big smile he said, "You bet! A lot less screaming!" You have to know kids really well to be there like that.

Seymour's behaviorist techniques represent one kind of "fundraising." Joyce's spontaneous knowing and responding represents another kind (an *I–Thou*-ish kind) of putting money in the bank. Regardless of your teaching philosophy, *we need to put money in the bank*. In order to teach, we need to make deposits. Do it with techniques. Do it with your whole self saying "I."

Start every class with personal greetings—and remember that greeting goes far beyond "hello."

TEACHING JEWISHLY

KAVOD HA-TALMID— RESPECT FOR STUDENTS

Hevruta Study

THE TORAH SOURCE

AND MOSHE SAID TO YEHOSHUA: "CHOOSE FOR US MEN, AND GO TO FIGHT WITH AMALEK."

Exodus 17.9

Rashi comments: "CHOOSE FOR US." Moses uses "us," making Yehoshua his equal. From this insight the Sages have said, "Let the honor of your student be as dear to you as your own honor."

Shulḥan Arukh, Yorah Daiah 242.33

RESPECT FOR STUDENTS IS RESPECT FOR GOD

One who pays respect to others, it is just like that one was paying respect to the Divine Presence.

Jerusalem Talmud, Eruvin 5:1, 22a

EVERYONE DESERVES RESPECT

There is no one in the world who does not deserve some respect. One who pays respect to another by so doing respects him/herself, for respect creates respect, while disrespect re-echoes in disrespect. The greatest education that can be given to a child is that of respect, not only for his friends, parents, and relations, but also for the servants in the house. Once the Prophet Muhammad, hearing his grandson call a slave by his name, told him, "Call him Uncle, for he is advanced in years." If one wishes to respect someone, one will surely find something to respect in that person; and if there is nothing at all to be found, then the very fact that he is a human being quite entitles him/her to respect.

From *The Art of Being and Becoming*, Hazrat Inayat Khan

RESPECT REMOVES POWER STRUGGLES

When we offer kids a choice instead of making a demand, no power struggle ever begins. When we make a demand, we own the wise choice, leaving the child with only one way to win the power struggle—by making a foolish choice. Given a range of choices, a child has endless opportunities to choose wisely.

Jim Fay and David Funk, *Teaching with Love and Logic*

TWO STORIES ABOUT RABBI YISRAEL SALANTER

So careful was Rabbi Yisrael (Lipkin of Salant, founder of the Musar Movement) to honor others, he would even address young boys with the formal you (*Ihr*) in Yiddish in order to develop their self-esteem.

In a certain town there lived a poor student who went unnoticed by his townspeople. They did not recognize his true worth and did not trouble themselves about his financial straits. This scholar complained to Rabbi Yisrael who then traveled to the city to pay him a visit. When the townspeople saw the esteem Rabbi Yisrael accorded this student they realized that a great scholar was living among them.

Sparks of Mussar

A Little Musar

When Rabbi Akiva Eiger's children were preparing his responsa for publication, Rabbi Eiger wrote to them: "Among the responsa you will undoubtedly find many letters to those who have studied in my yeshiva. Please do not refer to them as my students, for I have never called anyone my student. How can I know who has learned more from whom?"

Introduction to T'shuvot Rav Akiva Eiger

In the last chapter we talked about *sever panim yafot,* greeting students with a cheerful countenance. We talked about how a simple greeting can set a tone for a relationship with each student. In this unit we are going to talk about extending that sense of greeting throughout the lesson by focusing on *kavod ha-talmid,* the honor of each student.

A Prologue

Begin by reading this reflection by the Rav, Rabbi Joseph B. Soloveitchik.

> Whether you are indebted to me as your teacher is a separate question. But I certainly am indebted to you as a teacher more than you are indebted to me as my students. Do you know why? Because a teacher always acquires more from his students than the students from the teacher. Our sages long ago declared: "I have learned much from my teachers, and from my colleagues more than from my teachers, but from my disciples more than from them all" [Ta'anit 7a]. Maimonides explained that just as "a small log can kindle a large one, the young student likewise enables the learned teacher to enhance his wisdom" [Hilkhot Talmud Torah 5:13].
>
> ...Quite often, when I prepare the *shiur,* I cannot find the right approach. I sit with the Gemara, but it is a difficult *sugya* [subject for study]...Sometimes, at night, I am completely in despair. When I come into the classroom and sit down with my students, I slowly begin to analyze the *sugya.* Suddenly a light goes on, like a light from some mysterious source, and I begin to understand why it was so difficult for me to prepare the *shiur* the night before. Somehow, my students always inspire me. Many

of my *shiurim* are products of this consultation with my students...When I was young I used to compete with my students. The *shiur* used to be more of a symposium than a lecture. I let every student express his own understanding of the *sugya*. Many times I admitted in the classroom that the student was right and I was wrong. All this sharpened my mind and turned the study of Torah into a romance.

Related by the Rav in response to a presentation in his
honor at the Yarhei Kallah, Boston, Mass., August 25, 1981

Honoring Students Is a Biblical Mitzvah

AND MOSHE SAID TO YEHOSHUA: "CHOOSE FOR US MEN, AND GO TO FIGHT WITH AMALEK."

Exodus 17.9

Rashi comments: "CHOOSE FOR US." Moses uses "us," making Yehoshua his equal. From this insight the Sages have said, "Let the honor of your student be as dear to you as your own honor."

Ad loc.

So how does one show respect to students? Much of teaching has been about robbing the dignity of students. Much of what we know about classrooms actually comes from factories. Teachers were the bosses, and students were the workers. Just think about a few of these images: (a) teachers in big desks with a third of the room set aside for them, (b) students in small desks usually sharing two-thirds of the room, (c) teachers maintaining control by embarrassing students who fail to respond to their orders, and (d) teachers shaping every minute of classroom time as a totally unshared experience.

The Traditional Jewish Classroom

Traditional Jewish learning took place in a very different environment. Here is one traditional form known as the *Beit Midrash* model. The *Beit Midrash* is "the house of study." It begins with students preparing a text with a *hevruta*, a study partner. *Hevruta* pairs read the text out loud. They work on its meaning. In dyads every student has a voice and a right to say what he or she believes a text means. Each voice is valuable.

> Traditional Jewish text study is about exploring different aspects of a text and wrestling with (considering, responding to, arguing with, riffing on) both what you find in the text and what you and your *hevruta* have to add. In this wrestling process, you and your *hevruta* are creating something new with this text. If you include any other commentators in your studying (whether ancient or contemporary), they, too, become part of your conversation.
>
> *TorahQuest* Guide to *Hevruta* Study

Having prepared the text, the class then gathers and goes over the source with their teacher. Sam Heilman describes this part of the learning this way. He says that *lernen* (traditional Jewish study) happens in four movements.

> The first of these consists of an *oral reading* of the text, usually by one person who is cued or echoed by the others who are with him...*Translation*, the second step, became necessary when Jews no longer were fluent in the primary languages...but it was always part of the necessary expansion of the sketchy text...*Explanation*, the third move, is the effort to briefly clarify the meaning of implications of what has been recited. During explanation, learners define questions and refine answers. They organize a text, determining where one object or *inyan* ends and another begins. They frame matters, detailing

what the Talmud (text) is trying to do. Finally, they provide short glosses or footnotes to what they have just recited... *Discussion*, the last move, allows for the broadest possible consideration of the text. Mirroring the give-and-take of the sages...(they) evaluate the significance of what they have read and debate its conclusions, digress to tell stories or ask and answer questions...The students' concerns and words merge with the issues and language of the Talmud (text) they reviewed. This is the ultimate step of the process, the point at which life and *lernen* become one.

Heilman, Samuel C. The People of the Book: Drama,
Fellowship and Religion, Chicago: The University of Chicago, 1983

The vision of a Jewish classroom is one where every voice and every opinion, every single question is honored and valued. It operates with the belief that it is a classroom where each person present adds to and influences the learning. While much of this book will be about classroom management strategies that honor and respect students, the truth is that this respect and valuing must be part of the active learning experience. There are lots of different teaching styles that work effectively, and not all classrooms need look like this one, but all Jewish classrooms should share the concern of respecting each and every student.

Laws of Respecting Students

When I am looking for good texts on almost any Jewish topic I use books by Zelig Pliskin. He is a master at mining the Jewish tradition, particularly for values-oriented material. He assembled a list of Jewish laws about teaching that describe the way teachers can show respect.

[1] If students do not understand, a teacher should not get angry—rather the teacher should repeat the lesson as many times as necessary until they understand.

Yad, Laws of Talmud Torah, 4:4, Yoreh De'ah 246:10,11

[2] A teacher can act angrily if their lack of learning comes from laziness. A teacher should be able to instill fear when necessary.

Ketubot 103b, Yad, Laws of Talmud Torah, 4:5, Yoreh De'ah 246: 11

[3] A teacher must be interested in more than the subject matter. A teacher should also be interested in the student's welfare. A teacher should help students with personal problems.

Shivti b'Bet ha-Shem pp. 16, 30

[4] A teacher should be impartial.

Shabbat 10b, Shivti b'Bet ha-Shem p. 33

[5] A teacher should admit his/her own mistakes.

Zevaḥim 101a, Shivti b'Bet ha-Shem p. 22

[6] A teacher should not make promises or threats that will not be kept.

Sukkah 58b, Shivti b'Bet ha-Shem p. 35

[7] A teacher should not use sarcasm or ridicule. A teacher should discipline in a quiet, dignified, and positive manner.

Bava Metzia 58b, Shivti b'Bet ha-Shem p. 32

[8] A teacher must constantly learn.

Rashi on Exodus 4.1-3
Love Your Neighbor, Zelig Pliskin, (Aish haTorah Publications, 1977)

Techniques for Implementing Love and Logic

When it comes to the idea of "non-toxic" classroom management, my hero is Jim Fay, a parent and teacher trainer who runs the Love and Logic Institute out of Denver. He is a master at seeing ways for teachers to treat students with respect and in a growthful manner.

Love allows children to grow through their mistakes.
Logic allows them to live with the consequences of their

choices. The solutions offered through Love and Logic are based on these four principles:

Shared control—Teachers gain control by giving away the control they don't need.

Shared thinking and decision-making—Teachers provide opportunities for children to do the greatest amount of thinking and decision-making.

Equal shares of consequence and empathy—An absence of teacher anger causes a child to think and learn from his or her mistakes.

Maintaining a child's self-concept—Improved self-concept leads to improved behavior and improved achievement.

From *Teaching with Love and Logic* by Jim Fay and David Funk

In future chapters we will look at "embarrassment-free classrooms," "classrooms that build self-esteem," "the power of an apology," and engaging every student, dealing with special needs and other topics, all of which find their roots in this chapter.

TOKHEHAH—
THE ART OF SAYING "NO"

Hevruta Study

BIBLICAL MITZVAH

YOU MUST NOT HATE YOUR BROTHER/SISTER IN YOUR HEART
YOU MUST CERTAINLY REBUKE YOUR NEIGHBOR
AND NOT BEAR SIN BECAUSE OF THEM.

Leviticus 19:17

Why does the Torah add the phase "...AND NOT BEAR SIN
BECAUSE OF THEM" to the end of this verse? To teach us not
to embarrass in others in public when we rebuke them.

Rashi, ad loc.

WHO SHOULD NOT BE REBUKED?

Rabbi El'a further stated in the name of Rabbi Elazar, son
of Rabbi Shimon: "Just as it is a mitzvah to say that which
will be listened to, so it is a mitzvah not to say that which
will not be listened to."

Abba stated: Both are obligations, for the Bible teaches,
"DON'T REBUKE A SCOFFER, FOR THEY WILL HATE YOU;
REBUKE A SAGE AND THEY WILL LOVE YOU" *(Proverbs 9:8)*.

Talmud Bavli, Yevamot 65b

When to Rebuke, How to Rebuke

If a person sees another has sinned or is following a bad way, it is a mitzvah to attempt to return them to the right way and to inform them that they are sinning against themselves in their evil deeds, as it says: "You must certainly rebuke your neighbor" *(Leviticus 19:17)*.

One who rebukes another person, whether for a wrong committed between the two of them or between the other and God, should give rebuke privately. They should speak to them patiently and gently, informing them that they are only making these statements for their welfare, to allow them to merit the life of the world to come. If they accept the rebuke, fine. If not, they should be rebuked a second time and a third. Indeed, one is obligated to rebuke another person who does wrong until they strike them and tell them: "I will not listen." And whoever is able to rebuke and does not is somewhat responsible for the sin, because they could have given rebuke.

Maimonides: *Laws of Character* 6:7

Before assuming that a person deserves *tokhehah*, reproof, for his/her actions one must be absolutely certain that s/he has, in fact, sinned. From the command, "Judge your fellow favorably" *(Leviticus 19:15)*, we learn that if a person appears to be committing a transgression which is totally out of character for him, we are to seek to understand what transpired in a positive light. If there is any way to interpret his actions as not involving transgression, we are required to do so. If it is absolutely clear that the person did sin in a manner that is out of character for him, then we must assume that he immediately regretted the actions and has already repented. To discuss the incident with anyone constitutes speaking *lashon ha-ra*.

Chofetz Chayim

How Many Times Should You Try?

From where do we learn that one who has rebuked four and five times should rebuke again? It is written: "YOU MUST CERTAINLY REBUKE..." *(Leviticus 19:17)*.

Sifra, Kedoshim 2:84

A Spiritual Guide to Rebuking

Said the Baal Shem Tov: "One who sees faults in another and dislikes the other because of them definitely has some of the same faults in his/her own person. The pure and good person can see only the goodness in others. We read: 'YOU SHOULD NOT HATE YOUR BROTHER IN YOUR HEART; YOU SHOULD CERTAINLY REBUKE YOUR NEIGHBOR, AND NOT BEAR SIN BECAUSE OF THEM' *(Leviticus 19:17)*. This teaches us: Rebuke yourself first for seeing faults, and thus being to a degree impure; then you will not hate your sister, but feel love towards her. If you rebuke her, it will be in the spirit of love. She will become attached to you, joining the goodness within her to your own goodness, and all her faults will disappear."

The Hasidic Anthology, L. Newman

Jewish Classroom Management: Gentle Control

Much of what a teacher does is tell students that they are wrong. Correction is a big part of teaching. We tell students that they are not solving problems correctly, not reading a passage correctly, not getting the answers right. And when it comes to behavior, we often have to "correct" and modify that, too.

Much of secular education literature about classroom management is about structured embarrassment of students. Whether we are calling them by name, yelling to scare them straight, or stealthily making checks on the blackboard, we usually use embarrassment or fear of embarrassment to keep our students in line. We start by calling the child by name whose behavior we want to modify. We convince ourselves this is a way of grabbing the student's attention. So we say nicely, "Roger, will you please sit down?" If we are good, we say it politely and gently. But the truth is that when we say "Roger, will you please sit down?" the class often hears and knows that "Roger isn't sitting down again." We continue to use the student's name, we speak louder and louder—we create a drama in the classroom that focuses attention on the student whose behavior needs to conform. We dare them to flinch first. The process is simple—embarrassment is used to modify behavior.

Here is the problem. Embarrassment is an effective way of controlling many situations, but Jewish values forbid embarrassment—or at least insist that we create minimal embarrassment. Now, starting with this chapter, we will begin to look at how we can show respect and minimize embarrassment when we need to intervene in behavior. Various Jewish legal authorities give teachers the ability to use embarrassment when absolutely necessary.

Giving negative feedback while retaining the other's respect is a big Jewish topic. It is a biblical mitzvah. In the Torah we are told,

YOU MUST NOT HATE YOUR BROTHER/SISTER IN YOUR HEART.

YOU MUST CERTAINLY REBUKE YOUR NEIGHBOR

AND NOT BEAR SIN BECAUSE OF THEM (Leviticus 19.17).

Rashi comments on this verse and says, "Why does the Torah add the phase, '...AND NOT BEAR SIN BECAUSE OF THEM' to the end of this mitzvah? To teach us not to embarrass others in public when we rebuke them."

The Hebrew word for rebuke is *tokhehah*. There are a lot of *tokhehah* rules. When we look at them, a model for managing a classroom Jewishly emerges.

1. *Tokhehah* must be given out of love, not out of anger. It is designed to help the other person change.

   PROOFTEXT: Speak pleasantly and softly when you admonish someone. Explain to the person that you have only his/her benefit in mind.

   Rambam, *Hilkhot Deyot* 6.7

2. *Tokhehah* must not be embarrassing.

   PROOFTEXT: Someone once reported to Rabbi Noson Tzvi Finkel how he had rebuked a wrongdoer very sharply. "I wasn't able to effect a change in that person," he said. "But at least I made his face turn red as a beet." This greatly irritated Rabbi Finkel, and he commented, "Our Sages (Arahin 16b) explain that the verse 'REBUKE YOUR NEIGHBOR' is followed by the verse 'DO NOT BEAR SIN BECAUSE OF YOUR NEIGHBOR' to teach us that even when rebuking others, we are forbidden to embarrass them. Yet you are proud that you humiliated someone!"

   T'nuat ha-Mussar, vol. 3, p. 258

3. *Tokhehah* should strive to make a positive change in the other person. It should be done in a manner that will be heard and in a manner that enables change.

PROOFTEXTS: When rebuking someone, do not tell him that he is wicked or evil. Instead, elevate her and explain that someone of her stature should behave differently. In this manner your admonition is apt to be successful.

Havot Yair, cited in *Maayoneh Shel Torah*

Even when you rebuke someone privately, you must be very careful not to shame him or her.

Rambam, *Hilkhot Deyot* 6:8

Each situation is different, and to prevent someone from doing wrong the method must fit the particular person involved. Before admonishing someone, offer a prayer that your admonition should be delivered in a manner that will be effective.

Marganita Tava, no. 13

4. Anger will prevent *tokhehah* from being heard. When a person hears anger in another person's voice, the person responds defensively, often with his or her own anger. Anger will not get people to think. Anger will only get people to respond emotionally. That is not a good place to be when you want to discuss change.

PROOFTEXTS: You must be very careful not to grow angry when rebuking someone.

Marganita Tava no. 10

Rebuke delivered in anger will not be heeded.

Erekh Apayim p. 44

Rabbi Hayyim of Volozhin said that if a person is unable to admonish others in a pleasant tone of voice, s/he is exempt from the obligation to deliver *tokhehah.*

Keser Rosh, no. 143; *Minhat Shmuel,* p. 34

5. You are not allowed to give up hope of someone changing.

> **PROOFTEXT:** The Chofetz Chayim gives an analogy to a person who sells apples. He will keep calling out "Apples for sale!" the entire day. Even if one passerby in a hundred heeds his sales pitch, it is worthwhile. This is his livelihood, and he cannot afford to remain silent.
>
> The same is true of rebuke. Of course, a person does not always effect a change in the recipient of his rebuke. But even if one is successful only occasionally, it is worth his efforts.
>
> Chofetz Chayim, Al ha-Torah

Relatively Embarrassment-Free Techniques of Classroom Management

These are the strategies that will modify behavior in a low-impact way. It is possible that not even the student you are singling out will know that you are focusing on his/her behavior.

- **The General Announcement:** The first step in modifying behavior is to politely ask the whole class to change their behavior even if one only one person needs to be acting differently: "Could I please have everyone quiet down?" "I need everyone quiet, please."

  And then there is that great camp technique for younger classrooms: "If you can hear me, clap once." "If you can hear me, clap twice," etc., until the room is quiet. Having no specific target for a behavior reminder prevents anyone from feeling singled out.

  REMEMBER: Tone is really important. You want to be soft and gentle. The idea is that you want to control your room without ever breaking a sweat.

- **The Teacher Look (Evil Eye):** If you've been in the classroom, you should already have this one down. It is catching the eye of the student in question and giving a look of disapproval.

- **Eye Contact Targets Student, Head Shake Reveals Intent:** This is the "evil eye," level two. Make eye contact. Give a quick shake "No!"

- **The Zone Defense:** This one is easy. If a child is misbehaving, you can often modify his/her behavior by just moving in close to her/him. Teachers who regularly move around the room can position themselves close to, or even behind, a student who's talking or passing notes, etc. The presence of a teacher can often halt this behavior without a word needing to be said. If necessary, the teacher can even teach from that part of the room for a while. Meanwhile, nothing is said to or about the student.

Low-Embarrassment Techniques

This set of techniques may cause some embarrassment, but the amount is minimal. It is a lot less than would take place through a traditional management process.

- **Providing Choices:** It is always better to offer choices when you can. For instance, if you have to move someone's seat, it is far better to say, "I'm sorry, but I'm going to have to move you. Would you like to sit over here or over there?" We will talk a lot more about moving seats later. Choices are good. They share power and control with the student.

- **The Student Whisperer:** One great way of asking a student to stop (or start) doing something is to lean down and whisper. Whispering is good for two reasons. First of all, a whisper has no affect, so there is no chance that a student will take your intervention as anger. Second, a whisper gives the illusion of privacy. It lets both the student involved and the other students believe that the interchange is private (not public). Among the things you could whisper are: "Could you please stop X?" "Could you save that for dance class?" (unless you are the dance teacher). With this, if you get a laugh, you've won. You can also ask, "Is that the right place for that?"

- **Cool Time-Out Space:** Create a cool time-out space. Jim Fay tells the story of a teacher who brought in a blanket and a beach umbrella and set up a little private corner. When a student seemed to be "losing it" the teacher would ask, "Could you use a little beach time?" This was not so much a punishment as a break from the pressures of the class. This teacher allowed students to opt for their own beach moments. Consider creating your own version (maybe a trip to Israel).

Higher-Embarrassment Options Done with Less Embarrassment

- **"I" Messages:** "I" messages are a key part of respectful, assertive speaking that allows us to express negative feelings without attacking or blaming. This is the difference between a **"you" message** and an **"I" message**:

  "You" message: "You are driving me crazy with your pencil tapping."

  "I" message: "I find it hard to teach when someone is tapping a pencil."

- **The Most Dangerous Classroom Move.** One of the most dangerous but necessary things we can do as classroom teachers is to move a student's seat. It may well be the most effective way to break a behavior pattern, but it is also the activity most likely to invite a student to say "No!" or to challenge our authority in other ways. Here are three strategies that minimize the dangers and keep a student from getting into a situation where he or she embarrasses him/herself. It is another Jewish value (*lifnai ever lo timshol,* not putting a stumbling block before the blind) that keeps us from setting up students to lose their tempers and embarrass themselves.

a. We have already discussed offering choices.

b. I once learned from a teacher in a workshop I was giving (I'm sorry I no longer remember her name to give her credit) that she regularly moves students around in her classroom. She regularly arranges new parings and new groupings. When she needs to move a student's seat it is no big deal, because students are moving seats all the time.

c. Think of the kid's defense "I know you are, but what am I?" The bully calls the kid another name, the kid repeats, "I know you are, but what am I?" The bully has to keep on thinking of new responses; the victim only needs to remember "I know you are, but what am I?" When the bully runs out of words, he (or she) walks away. We can use the same strategy in moving a student to another chair. Limit your vocabulary to four short sentences.

(1) Will you please move?

(2) Did I ask you nicely?

(3) Probably so.

(4) Nice try!

No matter how the student you are asking to move responds, your only response is one of these four sentences. Each time the student needs to think of a new response, you have only to choose from a limited vocabulary. Odds are that the student is going to run out of words and give up rather than be embarrassed by having nothing else to say.

It works like this:

"Roger, will you please move over there?"

"Jimmy was talking, too."

"Probably so. (Pause) Will you please move?"

"That's not fair."

"Probably so, but did I ask you nicely?"

"Yes."

"Then would you please move..."

...and so it goes. Odds are that the student is going to give up before the teacher, who all through this uses a soft, calm tone without a trace of anger, without showing any doubt that this situation will be resolved. Experience teaches that the rest of the class gives the teacher credit for having solved this problem calmly and without drama. This limited-response interaction is yet another Jim Fay idea.

- **Removing a Student from a Room:** The greatest chance a student will make a scene and embarrass him/herself is when you remove him/her from the room. I call this (politically incorrectly) "the kill shot," the painless way of removing a student from a room.

Something has gone on in your class that has triggered the need to send a child out of the room. Step One: Back off the confrontation.

Step Two: Ask yourself, "Do I have a *madrikh/madrikhah* (high school teaching assistant) in the room?" If the answer is yes, you are on the way to a solution. If the answer is no, you get question two, "Which student do you most trust to leave the room and run an errand?" One way or the other, you now have your messenger.

Step Three: Turn to your representative and say the following: "Please go to the office and tell _____ (fill in the principal's name) that I need to see him/her."

Step Four: Go back to your lesson. Your problem child will be quiet, hoping that s/he has escaped.

Step Five: When the principal arrives, say to him/her, "Roger needs to talk with you." At that point Roger leaves the room, and there has been no fuss. Roger may not appreciate this, but the rest of your class will.

Speaking in Private

Here is another secret. This one comes from all the literature in the Jewish tradition about *tokhehah*. Maimonides teaches:

> One who rebukes another person, whether for a wrong committed between the two of them or between the other and God, should give rebuke privately. The rebuker should speak to the person patiently and gently, informing the person that these statements of rebuke are only for his or her welfare...If the person accepts the rebuke, fine. If not, the person should be rebuked a second time and a third. Indeed, one is obligated to rebuke another person who does wrong until he or she strikes them and tells him or her: "I will not listen." And whoever is able to give rebuke and does not is somewhat responsible for the sin, because he or she could have given rebuke.
>
> (Maimonides, *Mishneh Torah, Book of Knowledge*, chapter 6.6,7)

Learn the words "Let's talk for a minute before you go out to recess." Or "See me for a moment after class, please." These are the first key to the best kind of teacher–student conversation. The less *tokhehah* that takes place in front of the class, the better. If you can in any way tolerate a behavior until there is a break, tolerate it and have a private conversation afterwards.

Once you've got the private moment, take the rest of Maimonides' advice. Speak patiently and gently. Make it clear that this is being done for the student's benefit, not for yours. And do not give up on the student. Behavioral change often takes more than one try.

Summing Up Rebuke

The basic idea of this chapter is simple: Teachers need to protect their students. Part of this comes through making the classroom an orderly and safe place. This happens through helping students conform to the behavioral standards of the learning community. It also happens through protecting the students from the teacher's worst instincts. Building a community based on trust allows a teacher to give a student feedback and have it be both safe and growthful. The idea is simple: Protect student dignity and gain trust. This applies not only to matters of classroom management. Consider:

- Calling on daydreaming students to embarrass them into paying attention

- Using a derogatory nickname for a student

- Sarcasm

All of this is rooted in the *Pirkei Avot* maxim (2.12):

Let other's honor be as dear to you as your own.

TEACH YOUR CHILDREN WELL

Hevruta Study

OUR STUDENTS ARE LIKE OUR CHILDREN

And Abram took Sarai his wife, and Lot his brother's son and all their possessions that they acquired, and <u>the souls that they had made</u> in Haran, and they set out for the Land of Canaan.

Genesis 12.5

Rashi: Abraham taught Torah to and converted the men, and Sarah taught Torah to and converted the women. The Torah therefore credits Abraham and Sarah with making them, as it is written "THAT THEY HAD MADE."

Ad loc.

Resh Lakish said: "One who teaches Torah to a neighbor's child is regarded by the Torah as though s/he had given birth to the child, as it is written, 'AND THE SOULS <u>THAT THEY HAD MADE</u> IN HARAN.'"

Genesis 12.5

Rabbi. Eliezar said: "It is as though the Torah teacher had created the words of the Torah, as it is written, 'KEEP THEREFORE THE WORDS OF THIS COVENANT, <u>AND MAKE THEM</u>.'"

Deuteronomy 29.9

Rava said: "It is as though the Torah teacher had created him/herself, for it is written, 'AND MAKE THEM': translate the Deuteronomy verse not as 'THEM' but as 'YOURSELVES.'"

Sanhedrin 99b

TEACHERS ARE PARENTAL SURROGATES

Rabbi Judah taught us that Rav taught him this history lesson: "Rav said, 'The name of the man who is to be blessed is Yehoshua ben Gamla. Were it not for him, the Jewish people would have lost the Torah.

'In the beginning, every son was taught by his own father. If a boy had no father, he did not learn.' (*Formal Jewish education in the Rabbinic Era was only for boys. There is nothing we can do about that. The positive side of the story is that it was universal and paid for by the community.*)

Where in the Torah did they learn this practice? They learned this practice from Deuteronomy 11.19: "AND YOU SHALL TEACH THEM TO YOUR CHILDREN...." This practice emphasized the word אֹתָם (*otam*), "YOUR". In the Torah the word אֹתָם [*otam*] is written without a *vav*, and can be also be read as אַתֶּם [*atem*]. When you do that, the translation of וְלִמַּדְתֶּם אַתֶּם אֶת-בְּנֵיכֶם [*v'limmaditem atem et b'naikhem*] becomes: "AND YOU "<u>YOURSELF</u>" SHALL TEACH THEM...."

When this practice proved ineffective because it left out lots of children who did not have fathers who could do the job, the TANA'IM (the Rabbis of the Mishnah) ruled that teachers of young children should be appointed in Jerusalem so that any young person could go there and learn...

When this was put into practice there was still a problem. If a child had a father, the father would take him up to Jerusalem and have him taught there. But if he did not have a father, he would not go up and learn. The Rabbis of the

Mishnah therefore ruled that teachers should be appointed in each prefecture (Roman administrative district) and that boys should enter school at the age of sixteen or seventeen.

But this still didn't work well, because when teachers tried to discipline students that old, the students would rebel and then leave school. This is when Yehoshua ben Gamla ruled: "Teachers of young children should be appointed in each district and each town. This makes it possible for children to enter school at the age of six or seven."

Bava Batra 20b

YOUR STUDENTS ARE THE BUILDERS

Rabbi Eleazar said in the name of Rabbi Ḥanina: The students of the wise increase peace in the world, as it says, AND ALL YOUR CHILDREN SHALL BE TAUGHT OF THE ETERNAL, AND GREAT SHALL BE THE PEACE OF YOUR CHILDREN *(Isaiah 54.13)*. Read not בָּנָיִךְ *banayik* [YOUR CHILDREN] but בּוֹנָיִךְ *bonayik* [your builders].

Brakhot 64a

This chapter happened because I sent out a sketch of the previous chapter on the Torah Aura Bulletin Board and received this e-mail:

Many of us in small schools end up teaching our own children. It is a joke in my faculty that one should never teach one's own kid—but despite unbelievable juggling, every year one of us gets one of our own kids in class. This year in the eleven-twelve group is my son. When he studies the Earth moves, but when he goofs off—*oy vey*—it feels like the class is taking bets on who will come out on top, him or me...I try avoiding power struggles, but...What to do?

The first thing I did was talk to Carol Starin, who put this question out to her "five things crew." Here is some of the wisdom they shared.

[1] Years ago, when I was still in NY, my eighth-grade daughter was in my class. There is no question that she and her friends made my life miserable. I'm still not sure if it was because she was an eighth grader or because her mother was her teacher.

We are not a small school, but because I offer a choice of family classes or non-family classes, and because the vast majority of my teachers are congregants, I often have children who are in their parents' classes. The parent/teacher has a serious conversation with the child at the beginning of the year, explaining that there can be no special treatment and that there will also be no singling out that child for negative reasons. The parent and child agree that as much as possible they will treat each other as any teacher/student treat each other. If necessary, I review the rules with both the parent and the child. It's hardest with the little ones—the first place it's possible for this situation to happen in my school is with first grade. We tell the kids that when they are here, their mom or dad is their teacher and not Mom or Dad. Most of the time it works.

It's always interesting to read the report-card comments that a parent writes for his/her own child. They are always accurate and on target.

And, as in everything else we do, we treat each problem that might arise as an individual situation and find ways to deal with it (even if it involves the teaching parent asking for help with his or her own child from the non-teaching husband or wife).

[2] Having taught my daughter in preschool and one of my sons in seventh grade, I've had some personal experience. Regarding the preschooler, I had a good relationship with my assistant, and we agreed that she should handle most of the discipline issues regarding Laura as they arose. In our case that worked out very well, and Laura learned to trust and listen to another responsible adult. Richard, who was then the seventh grader, begged me to teach his class. He and I talked before the school year started and developed some ground rules, such as treating each other with mutual respect and clarifying our expectations (both behavioral and work-wise) of each other. I tried very hard to be fair with him and not single him out. I also expected him to play fair with me. The school principal stood ready to assist if necessary. It worked out just fine. The classroom teacher shouldn't hesitate to call on the principal if there are problems. Hope this is helpful. **Beth**

[3] It is going to depend (obviously) on the age of the child and the relationship between that specific parent and child. My wife taught our daughter in Sunday school in the first grade, and Lily was provided with content and structure appropriate to her age without any conflicts. Later, in sixth grade, I taught Lily again, and by this time she was an able critic of my teaching methods and skills…so my class improved. When it came to bat mitzvah, I couldn't tutor her, because I was THE TEMPLE tutor, so Rabbi

Magid wisely took over that role, and she did fine because she wasn't under pressure from me. I couldn't imagine what it was like to be the child of the bar/bat mitzvah tutor...my *mishugas*. So it all depends. **Daniel Bender**

[4] If parent conferences are necessary (as a regularly scheduled thing or as a consequence of troubling behavior), the other parent needs to be there. The teaching parent and child probably have to be good at being "teacher/student" during school more than "parent/child". **Debi Rowe**

The basic ideas here are simple. First, second, and third is the need for parents and children to talk, establishing the ground rules for being teacher and student. In addition, our expert panel talked about the availability of resources, classroom *madrikhim* and the principal. All of this is good wisdom.

There is, however, a second truth, one that we will explore over the next several chapters. While "transference" between parent and child can always turn into a problem, the truth is that certain kinds of classroom management styles will work better with your own children, and by in large those are the ones we are going to be exploring here. In figuring out how to be good to all students, especially all difficult students, you even give your own child the space to have difficult moments—and that is what a parent who is a teacher should do. The Talmud understands that and leaves us with this truth:

> If one lost something and one's parent lost something, the search for his/her own object takes precedence. Between one's own lost object and one's teacher's lost object, one's own takes precedence; but between one's parent's lost object and one's teacher's, one's teacher's takes precedence, because a parent brought you into this world, but a teacher who instructed one in wisdom brings

a student to the future world. But if a parent is a teacher, the parent takes precedence.

Bava Metzia 33a

Parent-teachers can be an ideal.

TEACHING JEWISHLY

T'SHUVAH—
REPENTANCE AND
THE CLASSROOM

Hevruta Study

Here is most of the seventh chapter of Maimonides' Mishneh Torah writing on repentance.

MISHNEH TORAH—LAWS OF REPENTANCE: CHAPTER SEVEN

1. Since free choice is granted to all people, a person should always strive to do *t'shuvah* and to confess verbally for sins, striving to cleanse his/her hands from sin in order that s/he may die as a *Baal-T'shuvah* (Master of Repentance) and merit the life of the world to come.

2. People should always see themselves as leaning toward death, with the possibility that they might die at any time. Thus they are afraid that they may be found sinners. Therefore, one should always repent of sins immediately and should not say "When I grow older, I will repent," for perhaps they will die before they grow older.

3. A person should not think that repentance is necessary only for those sins that involve deeds such as sexual impropriety, robbery, or theft. Rather, just as a person is obligated to repent of these, a person must search after the evil qualities s/he has. People must repent of anger, hatred, envy, frivolity, the pursuit of money and honor, the pursuit of gluttony, and the like…These sins are more difficult than

those that involve deeds. If a person is addicted to these behaviors, it is more difficult to separate from them.

4. A *Baal-T'shuvah* (a person who has repented) should not consider him/herself far below the level of the righteous because of the sins and transgressions that he or she committed. This is not true. He or she is loved and desired by the Creator as if he or she never sinned.

5. All the prophets commanded [the people] to repent. Israel will only be redeemed through *t'shuvah*.

6. *T'shuvah* is great, for it draws a person close to the *Shekhinah* (the part of God that gets close to people) as [Hoshea 14.21] states: "RETURN, O ISRAEL, TO YOUR GOD"... and [Jeremiah 4.1] states: "'IF YOU WILL RETURN, O ISRAEL,' DECLARES GOD, 'YOU WILL RETURN TO ME.'" Put them together, and you learn that if you will return in *t'shuvah*, you will be close to Me. *T'shuvah* brings near those who were far removed.

7. How high is the level of one who does *t'shuvah*! Previously the person who did wrong was separate from God, as [Isaiah 59.2] says: "YOUR SINS SEPARATE BETWEEN YOU AND YOUR GOD."...Now that person is clinging to the *Shekhinah*, as [Deuteronomy 4:4] states: "AND YOU WHO CLING TO GOD."

8. The manner of *Baalei T'shuvah* is to be very humble and modest. If fools shame them because of their previous deeds, the *Baalei T'shuvah*, they will hear this abuse and rejoice, knowing that it is a merit for them.

It is a total sin to tell *Baalei T'shuvah*, "Remember your previous deeds," or to recall them in their presence to embarrass them or to mention the surrounding circumstances or other similar matters so that they will recall what they did.

In the previous chapters we dealt with minor issues in classroom management. It was all about being kind and respectful when we modified small behaviors. In this chapter we are going to talk about dealing with a whole different magnitude of behavior. This chapter is not about a little talking or note passing, about pencil tapping or not sitting still. This is the chapter that goes to fighting and bullying, cheating and stealing, and to rudeness, attitude, and other real "discipline" issues.

The chapter is three pieces of background and then some technique.

Idea One: The *Yetzer ha-Ra*, the Source of Evil

AND YOU SHALL LOVE THE ETERNAL, YOUR GOD, **WITH ALL YOUR HEART**, AND WITH ALL YOUR SOUL, AND WITH ALL YOUR MEANS.

Deuteronomy 6.5

RASHI: "with all your **heart**." *What does it mean to love God with all your heart?* It means that you must love God with both of your drives, the drive toward good and the drive toward evil…

Sifrei 32 and Talmud, Brakhot 54a

Everyone can picture the cartoons that have a person with a devil on one shoulder and an angel on the other shoulder. Each of these "inner voices" speaks to the brain, trying to get the person to act in its direction. Judaism starts with this experience of being pulled two ways at once as one truth. The inner voice that tugs us toward the good is called the *yetzer ha-tov*, the good inclination. The other voice, the one that urges us toward the bad, is called the *yetzer ha-ra*, the evil inclination. Where Jewish thought differs from the classic cartoons (and much popular thinking) is that for us, both of these "inclinations" are gifts from God. There is no sense of a devil.

In an interesting passage in the midrash, the Rabbis teach that the *yetzer ha-ra* (the evil urge) can be "VERY GOOD." The rabbis make it clear that everything God has given us is useful and necessary—and everything can be abused and misused. Anger can be constructive! Love can be toxic! What matters is *when* a feeling is allowed to control our actions and how much of a feeling is influencing our decisions at any given time. Every feeling and every tendency can be useful. If they are in balance and in control, they are good. If they are out of balance and out of control, they become evil.

There is a midrash that explains this with a very simple story. God once got angry at the way people were acting, so God confiscated the *yetzer ha-ra* (the evil one) and locked it away. All of a sudden, no more children were born. God had to set the *yetzer ha-ra* free.

The lesson here is simple: Feelings like love of food, sexual desire, anger, desire for control, ego, and the like—things that we usually consider the source of problems—are also the needed sources of great and necessary things. Our path toward goodness is not a question of purging parts of ourselves; it is not a question of building walls around pieces of who we are; rather, it is a job of establishing equilibrium.

As teachers we learn here that our job is to help our children find their own inner balance and help them find ways of limiting and controlling many of their own urges. We are successful when our children learn to limit their appetites and learn when to act and when not to act on their strong feelings.

Idea Two: The Nature of Children

Although the Godly soul enters with the circumcision or naming, and continues to grow throughout the years of education, it enters in the most complete manner only on

the occasion of bar/t mitzvah. It is from this point on that
the Jew is able to wage war with the *yetzer ha-ra*.

Tanya, ch. 9

Think of two-year-olds. They own two words, "mine" and "no."
A person with only "mine" and "no" is a pretty good definition
of people who are ruled by their *yetzer ha-ra* (dark side). While
Western culture has a romantic notion that children are born
innocent, the Jewish tradition believes just the opposite. The
Rabbis teach that children are born with their *yetzer ha-ra* intact,
while it takes thirteen years for them to grow and develop their
yetzer ha-tov (good side). That is why bar and bat mitzvah is
placed at thirteen. Our children are born masters of "mine" and
"no"—it takes about thirteen years of work on "sharing" and
"compromise" and "I'm sorry" to grow out their inherent capacity
for good. Bar mitzvah is when we take off the training wheels,
believing that our children now have the tools to balance their
yetzer ha-ra with their *yetzer ha-tov* and begin to be responsible
for their own actions.

The understanding here is not that children are "born in sin";
rather, it suggests that it takes time to grow patience, compassion,
sensitivity, and the other skills that balance out the "mine" (that
gives us a sense of self) and the "no" (that protects us).

The big lesson we can learn here is that teaching our children
to be good is a lot like teaching them to ride a bicycle. We start
slowly, guiding them, but then we need to let go and stand
around while they sway too far from side to side and even fall
down some—until they find their own balance. Just like helping
them learn to ride a bicycle, raising good children is a process of
slowly letting go while not going away.

Idea Three: Repentance Is the Cure

The *yetzer ha-ra* and "free will" go together. If we did not have the capacity to make the "wrong" choices, then our actions would be controlled. Because God wanted us free to act, God had to give us the capacity to be out of balance, to go the wrong way, to make really bad decisions. Otherwise it would be like driving at Autopia at Disneyland: We would have the illusion of driving but no real ability to choose a direction. We would have our own guiderail hidden under the car.

As a teacher you already understand this, because your children's behavior has proven this. While you believe in their goodness, you've seen them make bad choices, be out of balance, and lack some of the self-control they need. The metaphor of "evil" not being a tug away from the good but an inappropriate use of the necessary conforms to our experience, when we think about it.

One wonderful idea in the Talmud is that "God allows no disease before there is the possibility of a cure." It is a wonderful statement that everything can be fixed. There is never cause to give up. In this case, we are taught that God created *t'shuvah*, the ability to make a "turning point" and start over, as the antidote to the *yetzer ha-ra*. It works like this: In giving us free will, God created the *yetzer ha-ra*. To keep the *yetzer ha-ra* from overwhelming us (and leading us to destroy the world) God created *t'shuvah*. *T'shuvah* is the opportunity to learn from mistakes and grow ourselves in a different direction. *T'shuvah* works through four steps (according to a medieval scholar named Isaac Arama): (1) We admit that we were wrong. (2) We apologize both to God and to the people we wronged. (3) We fix whatever can be fixed. (4) We do the inner work necessary to change our responses to given stimuli. In other words, we make sure that if we are in the same or a similar situation, our actions will be different.

God aids us in this situation through (a) helping us to know when we are wrong by providing a set of standards we can use as a ruler, (b) hearing our apology, (c) giving us tools for reflecting and changing, and (d) lovingly promising to forgive us always, once we've done our part of the work. God can also be the inspiration and provide the strength necessary to do this work.

The midrash makes it clear that parents are supposed to be God's personal representatives to their children; so are teachers. In raising a child we act for God. Our job, knowing that they will outgrow our control and go off on their own, is to empower them to make good choices and act responsibly, kindly, caringly in the world. We know that our children have freedom, and there are limits to the effectiveness of the boundaries we can set. Our powers decay over time, so like God, we need to use *t'shuvah*, repentance, as our antidote.

T'shuvah as a Classroom Management System

Our job is to teach our students how (1) to be less-defensively wrong, (2) to apologize for and fix the harm they do, and (3) to reflect, understand, and change (from the inside) the way that they act. Our job is to help them build tools that will allow them to accept more and more freedom while acting more and more responsibly. And our job is to, like God, lovingly forgive them once they have done their part of the work.

We do this through conversation—and it is conversation that takes place calmly, in quiet. Our job here is to coach, not to be Torquemada. Therefore we need to establish a place and a moment where conversation can take place.

0. Remember everything we have learned about *tokhehah*. It has to be clear that this is a conversation that is geared toward benefiting the student, not the teacher. Remember all the hints about speaking pleasantly, starting out with

empathy, not directly confronting, and expressing concern, not condescension.

1. Now think about Isaac Arama's four steps to *t'shuvah*. You are going to turn them into questions. The first: "What did you do wrong?" (Translation: Who got hurt by your actions?) Make sure that no "buts" are allowed. We will get to excuses (triggers) later. But for right now we are interested in the simple statement, "I was wrong when…" Not "I hit her after…"

2. The next question is "What do you have to do fix the situation?" Broken windows are easy. All you have to do is pay for them. Broken feelings are harder, because apologies don't fix the core problem, broken trust. Broken trust is a big issue. The only thing that fixes broken trust is time. One has to hang around long enough (with one's trustworthiness in question) until one finally earns back the trust. Learning how to fix broken feelings is a really useful skill.

3. The third question is an easier question: "To whom do you owe an apology?"

4. The fourth question is when the "but" kicks in. The fourth question is really two questions. (a) What caused you to lose control this time and act out? What was the trigger? (b) How are you going to stop yourself the next time this same trigger or one like it happens again? This is the learning self-control part. Here is where you as the teacher may need to make suggestions, but where the student ultimately must choose a strategy to change the way s/he acts. The student may not completely succeed the first time. (That would be complete repentance! And most of us never get there.) Being able to control this behavior most of the time would be a great improvement. And that is what we are aiming for.

This is a difficult route. It is much easier just to set limits, be welcoming, and not go through all this. But teaching your students how to be wrong and to change may be the greatest gift you can give them. It is not only a profoundly Jewish message, but also a most useful life skill. Because you are a Jewish teacher, this may be the single greatest gift you can give your students, because this is one of those places where Judaism meets real life and makes a difference.

Being a Role Model: An Afterword

Teachers are supposed to be good role models. Everything in this book creates a path toward the "*dugma* (good role modeling) is dogma" school of building *menshlekheit* through modeling. But if I had to point out one thing teachers could do for students that would be huge, that would simply be being wrong when they are wrong. Role modeling how to be wrong is a major gift in a culture where everyone places blame rather than accept responsibility. Any teacher that lives these same four steps in his or her own life presents students with the living reality that one can be wrong, accept responsibility, and not die. The reality of repentance is only understood in context, and while our culture understands "recovery," it doesn't understand being wrong (without a "but"). Showing your students that mistakes can be fixed is a redemptive act. It brings *t'shuvah* into the world.

FACING BULLYING

Hevruta Study

The Baal Shem Tov was the first Hasidic rabbi, a very wise and respected man. Many people turned to him to learn how to live according to Torah and how to behave in a Jewish way. Rabbi Hayyim hated his teachings and wrote against them. A stranger came into the house of study. Rabbi Hayyim said to the stranger, "Who are you?" The stranger answered, "I am nothing but dust and ashes." Rabbi Hayyim then said, "I am nothing but dust and ashes, too." Rabbi Hayyim suddenly knew that the stranger was the Baal Shem. They shook hands. They never agreed with each other, but from then on they were always respectful to each other.

Retold from Tales of the Tzadikim

Rabbi Eliezer Gordon was the founder of the Telshe Yeshiva. Many non–Jews used to come and see him and ask him to pray for their welfare. Once a non–Jewish farmer came to him and asked him to pray that his enemy should die. Rabbi Gordon explained to the farmer that it was not right to curse his neighbor, but it was right to pray that his enemy should become his friend.

T'nuat ha-Mussar, vol 2. p. 433

Rabbi Rafael of Bershid was once visiting a certain town on *Tisha B'av* (a fast day commemorating the destruction of the Temple). He was brought in to mediate a bitter feud between two groups in town. He said, "Tell me about the feud." They said, "This can wait until tomorrow when the fast is over." He said, "We will begin today, because Jerusalem was destroyed by a feud that no one mediated."

Yoma 9b, the story of Kamza and Bar Kamza

Today is the right day to try to promote peace.

Midrash Pinḥas, p. 33b

Rabbi Isaac said: "One who offends a neighbor and does so only through words must pacify him...If the neighbor has a claim of money upon you, pay him/her, and if you cannot, send many friends to him/her."

Rabbi Ḥisda said, "One should try to pacify him through three groups of three people each."

Rabbi Yosi ben Ḥanina said, "One who asks pardon of his neighbor need do so no more than three times."

Rabbi Abba had a complaint against Rabbi Jeremiah. Rabbi Jeremiah went and sat down at the door of Rabbi Abba, and as the maid poured out water, some drops fell upon his head. Then he said: "They have made a dung-heap of me" (I Samuel 2.8). He quoted a passage about himself: "HE RAISES UP THE POOR OUT OF THE DUST." Rabbi Abba heard this and came out toward him, saying, "Now I must come forth to appease you, as it is written: 'GO, HUMBLE THYSELF AND URGE THY NEIGHBOR'" (Proverbs 6.3).

When Rabbi Zera had any complaint against any person, he would repeatedly pass by that person, showing himself, so that others could go forth to pacify him.

Rav once had a complaint against a certain butcher, and when on the eve of the Day of Atonement the butcher did not come to him to apologize, Rav said: "I shall go to him to make peace." Rabbi Huna met Rav and asked: "Where are you going?" Rav said, "To make peace." He thought: "Because the butcher had neglected to make his effort to reconcile, Rav is about to cause his death." But Rav went and remained standing before the butcher, who was sitting and chopping an animal's head. He raised his eyes and saw Rav, then said: "You are Rav, go away. I will have nothing to do with you." Whilst he was chopping the head a bone flew off, struck the butcher's throat, and killed him.

Talmud, Yoma 87a

Rabbi Yoshe Ber, the Rabbi of Brisk, once reprimanded a butcher for doing wrong. He pleaded with the man to change his ways, but the man refused. On the day before Yom Kippur Rabbi Ber went to the butcher and asked forgiveness. The butcher was surprised and said, "Why does the Rabbi ask my forgiveness? I should be asking forgiveness of you—because I did not listen to what you told me." The Rabbi answered, "That is why I have to ask your forgiveness, because when original words didn't make a difference, all I was doing was making myself feel proud about pointing out your faults. It was vanity." The butcher was so ashamed that he started to weep. He said he would do everything possible to change.

Rabbi A.Y. Kahn, The Taryag Mitzvot

Rav Abraham Isaac Kook: "There are those who mistakenly think that world peace can only come when there is a unity of opinions and character traits. Therefore, when scholars and students of Torah disagree and develop multiple approaches and methods, they think that they are causing strife and opposing shalom. In truth, it is not so, because true shalom is impossible without appreciating the value of pluralism intrinsic in shalom. The various pieces of peace come from a variety of approaches and methods that make it clear how much each one has a place and a value that complements another. Even those methods that appear superfluous or contradictory possess an element of truth that contributes to the mosaic of shalom. Indeed, in all the apparently disparate approaches lies the light of truth and justice, knowledge, fear and love of God, and the true light of Torah."

Rabbi Abraham Isaac, *Kuk Olat Re'iah*, Vol. 1

This chapter got started after the shooting at Santee High School that was part of the wave that followed Columbine. As the details of that story began to unfold it became an archetypal story: Kid is the victim of bullying, kid strikes back with "ultra-violence" and shoots students and faculty in his school. About the same time I found a book in a Jewish bookstore called *Shalom Secrets, A Child's Guide: How to Live in Peace with Friends and Family*. The book got me thinking that Judaism had some wisdom to teach about bullying. I began studying and reflecting. That reflection turned into a group activity called *Agents of Peace*. This chapter comes from that game, which Torah Aura Productions still sells.

Introduction

We are starting with a single understanding. Shawn Johnston, a psychologist in private practice in California, has specialized in working with violent youth. What he has to say is this: "The mental world of these young killers is all about 'me.' They're frustrated, angry, in some pain, not getting everything they want. They feel like victims. They have no concern about others—they don't think about others. It's all about who they are and what they want."

Dorothy Lewis, professor of psychiatry at NYU School of Medicine, says, "Probably the most powerful generator of aggression in living beings is pain... Animals that have been tortured and children who have been severely and repeatedly abused often become extremely aggressive. Animals and humans being raised in the company of violent adults is associated with the development of aggressive behavior patterns."

Charles Andrew Williams was the shooter in the killings at Santee High School in California. His friends set up a website for him,

http://www.friendsofandyw.org. On it a high school student, Hannah S., who served as a teaching assistant in his English class, wrote, "I wonder where the teachers were at when they were picking on him. I know that he should have turned for help instead of taking a stupid gun to school, but they picked and picked and picked and picked on him where he was pressured to do such a terrible thing. I know that was wrong, but they had no right to tease him about his clothes, about his ears, or about they way he walks, or stealing his stuff. That was way wrong just because he was from the country...those city kids had no right. I hope that Andy will be tried as a juvenile. It will give him time to learn his mistakes and to recuperate. My heart goes out to Andy and those that died and were injured."

When you begin to read the narratives created by the students who act out violently against their peers, it is easy to be overwhelmed by the amount of pain they feel that they have experienced at the hands of their fellow students. The simple truth is that if we can reduce bullying, if we can make our middle schools and our high schools less cruel, make them kinder and gentler communities, we can reduce the amount of violence that happens there.

Likewise, to see the pain of the victims of bullying, check out **www.jaredstory.com**. The simple truth is that both bullies and victims are at long-term risk. Victims wind up with low self-esteem and can develop eating disorders and addictions and commit suicide. Studies suggest that bullies, too, suffer. Bullying is often the passing on of abuse that the bully has received. Bullies grow up to have poor academic, work, and marital records and are equally at risk for problems with addiction.

Albert Einstein wrote:

> When a human being experiences himself, his thoughts and feelings, as separate from the rest of humankind, it is

a kind of optical delusion of consciousness. This delusion is a prison, restricting us to our personal desires and to affection for the few persons nearest us. Our task must be to free ourselves from this prison by widening our circle of compassion, to embrace all living creatures and the whole of nature in its beauty. Nobody is able to achieve this completely, but the striving for such an achievement is, in itself, a part of the liberation and foundation of our society.

That is the context of this work.

Teacher Truths

Bullying is one of the hardest things for teachers to deal with because it happens, for the most part, at times when the teacher is not there, or in ways that the teacher does not know. It is something we hear about, but for the most part we do not witness it. Or when we do see it, we see it as a series of minor incidents, not as a punishable offense.

When it all is boiled down, teachers have three paths of action. Each of them has limited potential, but they are the best tools we have.

- **Counseling the Bully.** All of the rules of loving *tokhehah* apply. Two things we know are that (a) the bully is likely to be the victim of bullying (bullying flows downhill); and (b) the bully, even more than the victim, is at risk. Studies show that bullies are at risk for criminal behavior, drug addiction, poor marriages, uncontrolled anger, etc. Bullying behavior is something we need to help people outgrow, not only for the victim's sake, but for their own.

- **Creating a Class Culture Against Bullying.** It is possible to teach against bullying. Most of this chapter will outline a way of doing that. So will Torah Aura's *Agents of Peace*. Much of it has to do with showing "ordinary" kids ways they can intervene in bullying situations. Our secret is going to be not confronting the bullies but rather supporting the victims.

- **Undermining the Bullies' Support.** To a large degree bullies need audiences. When you can separate them from their circle, the bullying often falls apart. This strategy, which we can also teach to kids, is to work with individual members of the crowd to get them to back off of their support of the bully.

Here is the truth: Bullying is something you can address before it ever happens. It can regularly become part of your curriculum. This chapter should give you some resources for doing that.

Being a *Rodef Shalom*—An Agent of Peace

A Jewish response to bullying starts with the value of *rodef shalom*. A *rodef shalom* is someone who chases after peace. In the book of Psalms (34.15) it says,

"SEEK PEACE AND CHASE IT."

Rabbi Yoḥanan explained that this text teaches that to have peace one should be like a helmsperson on a boat. "A person should always be on the lookout for an opportunity and then chase peace."

Leviticus Rabbah 21.5

If you read carefully, you will notice that there are two different behaviors being discussed here, "seeking peace" and "chasing peace." If you read the Torah with Rabbinic eyes, you automatically know that these two are not the same. In the commentaries it is made clear that seeking peace is going with options that are likely to lead to peace, whereas chasing peace is aggressively pursuing paths that might lead to peace. The first is going with paths that lead to peace; the second leads to making peace happen at times when it is not likely. Cases involving bullying often require us to go out of our way, not merely respond to extant situations. Often bullying calls upon us to create the fixes. Here is a Rabbinic example of making peace happen.

> Hillel used to say: "Be a student of Aaron, one who loves peace and chases peace..." *(Pirkei Avot 1.12)*

> When two people had an argument, Aaron would go and sit down with one of them and say: "Listen carefully to what your friend is saying! Your friend is feeling really sad. Your friend is saying, 'I have messed up! I am the one who was wrong. I don't even know what to say to my friend to begin to make up.'" Aaron would stay there until all the anger had passed from that person's heart. Aaron then would go and sit with the other person and say the same exact thing. He would sit with that second person until all the anger had passed from that person's heart, too. When the two met each other again, they would embrace and make up.

> *Pirkei Avot* According to Rabbi Nathan, chapter 12

Take a look at this last text. It sets up our conversation about bullying. It gives us a valid reason for negotiating with bullies, for looking for solutions even when they seem difficult.

> Seek peace with your friend and chase it with your enemy. Seek it in your place and chase in other places. Seek it with your body and chase it with your money. Seek it for yourself and chase it for others. Seek it today and chase it tomorrow. Never give up and say "I will never achieve peace," but chase it until you do.

> Yeḥil ben Yekutiel, *Sefer Maalot ha-Middot*

The bottom line learned from these three texts is a commitment to going out of one's way to create peace. It sets up a direction for our work will bullies. We are looking not only to use force (the teacher's authority) to fix the situation but to actually resolve the situation. Our job is to try to make things better.

Three Case Studies

Our exploration will use three cases to unpack a process. The first case is a family case, not a school case. It will help us deal with confrontation. The second case is a school bullying situation where we are facing a single bully. The third case is a summer camp case. It deals with a group that is picking on an individual. Out of these three cases and the texts emerges a series of steps, a process for dealing with bullies.

Case 1: Anna Borrows Shira's Clothes

One sister borrows another sister's clothing without permission. How should the first sister react? We offer four choices: (a) Telling a parent; (b) Nicely asking that her sister ask permission; (c) Very nicely asking that her sister ask permission; (d) Ignoring the problem for the moment.

Shalom bayit means "family peace." It is an important Jewish value. This text is one statement of its importance.

> His students once asked Rabbi Adda bar Ahavah, "What is the reason you've managed to live so long?" He answered, "Because I have never lost my temper with my family."
>
> Ta'anit 20b

This particular text suggests patience in dealing with a family member. The next text will generalize that patience, that forgiveness beyond the family to others.

> When the Holy One was ready to create people, the angels divided into two groups. One side said, "Let people be created," while the other said, "Let them not be created."

> This story is told in the book of Psalms, where it says, "LOVE AND TRUTH FOUGHT TOGETHER. RIGHTEOUSNESS AND PEACE BATTLED EACH OTHER" (Ps. 85.11). Here is what happened:

Love said, "Create people, because they will perform acts of love."

Truth said, "Don't create people, because they will all lie a lot."

Righteousness said, "Create people, because they will do righteous deeds"

Peace said, "Don't create people, because they will get into conflict after conflict."

What did the Holy One do? God took truth and buried it in the ground. Then God created people.

Genesis Rabbah 8.5

The idea is that to have peace, one must bury truth. As long as one holds on to truth there is always a need to get even. Truth breeds revenge. In order to make peace one has to abandon the desire to strike back, to get even, and to start the relationship anew. That, too, is an important truth. One-time incidents should not be the beginning of conflict. Justice and truth are not equal. That is why the example of the amnesty process in South Africa is such a powerful model. It lives this piece of midrash.

Keeping the Peace

Korakh was a relative of Moses. He started a big argument and tried to take over the leadership of the Jewish people. As part of this struggle for control many people were killed. After it was all over, God told Moses, "No one should ever act like Korakh."

No one was quite sure what was actually being forbidden. Different rabbis had different ideas.

Rabbi Joseph D. Epstein thought that it taught "It is bad to start an argument, but worse to continue it."

Mitzvot ha-Shalom, pp. 122–24

Rabbi Reuven Margolies taught that it means "One is never allowed to hate."

Magoliyot ha-Yom to Sanhedrin 110a, 6

Rabbi Zalman Nehemiah Goldberg taught that it means "One should never be the one who starts an argument— especially if one can prevent it by not worrying about being right and 'I'm sorry' first will prevent it." He adds that "In reality it doesn't matter who really did the wrong thing to begin with."

Moriah, vols. 169/170.62–72

Again we are underlining the notion that not every provocation is a call for action. This does not mean that bullying should be tolerated, but it does suggest that not every act of teasing is a pattern of continual provocation—and that every fight is the source of ongoing conflict. Patience both for students and for teachers is a useful step. The pause before action is critical. In the book of Proverbs (17.1) we are told:

Better a stale crust of bread with peace than a huge banquet with fighting.

In this case Shira has to choose between protecting the things that belong to her and preventing an argument with her sister.

The Best Jewish Answer: Ignore the situation for the moment. (We will learn more about how to revisit this problem with the sister in case three.) If *sh'lom bayit* is really a high-level priority, then the wearing of clothes is not a big enough deal to cause a fight. In addition, the Talmud does not understand individual family members having private possessions.

Case 2: Zack Bullies Ben

Jon sees Zack bullying Ben. He has four choices of how to react. (a) Ignoring the situation; (b) Telling a teacher; (c) Confronting Ben; (d) Telling Ben that he is not to blame.

Once again we turn to a collection of Jewish sources. This time we are going to see how the Jewish tradition focuses on the victim.

In the book of Psalms (145.15) we are told:

> GOD SUPPORTS THOSE WHO ARE FALLING AND LIFTS UP EVERYONE WHO IS BENT OVER.

In the prayer book we use those words and say:

> GOD LIFTS UP THOSE WHO ARE FALLING, HEALS THOSE WHO ARE SICK, AND RELEASES THOSE WHO ARE BEING HELD PRISONER...

We also learn in the Torah (Genesis 1)

> GOD CREATED PEOPLE "B'ZTELEM ELOHIM," IN GOD'S IMAGE.

In many ways Ben is falling. It is an emotional falling, but it is a falling. Similarly Ben is sick and Ben is being held prisoner. *Someykh noflim* is the Hebrew for "lifting up the falling." In this case Jon can be a *someykh noflim* for Ben. Our job is to help Jon learn about "lifting up the fallen." Here is a proactive mitzvah that could make a major difference in the impact of Zack's actions. They could be nullified by an act of caring.

In the Torah we are told (Leviticus 19.18):

> YOU MUST LOVE YOUR NEIGHBOR AS YOU LOVE YOURSELF.

Different rabbis have understood what kinds of things one should do for others in different ways. Here are a few of those ideas.

Rabbi Moses ben Maimon taught

> "This means we must praise other people, care about their money as much as we care about our own, and care about their feelings as much as we care about our own. God rejects anyone who builds honor through making fun of someone else."

> *Yad, Hilkhot De'ot 6.3*

The lesson for Jon is that he cannot walk away. While his obligation to confront Zack is problematic, he does have an obligation to protect Ben's feelings. Zack is clearly violating the mitzvah of "loving one's neighbor," and Jon has the obligation to make it better.

In a book called *Pele Yoatz*:

> "To love your neighbor as yourself, you must treat other people based on their feelings and not yours. If a person wants something done, even if you would not need it done if it was you, you do it for the one who wants it. Even if you would not mind if someone said something to you, you cannot say it to a person who would be bothered by it."
>
> Section Ahavah

The lesson here is that feelings belong to the other person. When figuring out how to act on another's feelings you must understand the person and not project your own feelings onto him or her. Zack's actions may be something you could just walk away from. The question that is important is not what you would do, but how does Ben feel?

In a book called *Orhot Tzadikim* there is a long list of things that are part of "loving your neighbor." Here are a few:

> "I should help others in every way possible according to my ability. I must not be strict with others in small matters. I always wish to make others happy and will always speak pleasantly to everyone. I will help others with their burdens but will not cause others trouble. I will not get into fights. I will greet every person with joy and a pleasant facial expression, for this will strengthen love. I will deal with others for their good. When others are sad and worried, I will comfort them. I should honor every person with deeds and with words. I should not act condescendingly towards anyone."
>
> Sha'ar Ahavah

This text expands the message given in the previous text. Our obligation to others involves helping them in most ways and causing no harm. It is a big "no man is an island" moment. It strengthens the list of obligations we get to teach about. This last set of texts may seem trivial, but they strengthen the proactive obligations we have to other people.

A lot of rabbis believe that saying hello, particularly with *Shalom* attached, is a mitzvah.

Some people learn it from Moses greeting Yitro, his father-in-law.

Exodus 18.7, Immrei Yehezkeil ad loc.

Some people learn it from Ya'akov asking about Lavan.

Genesis 29.6

Some people learn it from Yosef welcoming his brothers when they get to Egypt.

Genesis 43.27

The Talmud gives Boaz, the man who marries Ruth and takes care of Naomi, credit for making a greeting a mitzvah. We are taught that *Shalom* is one of God's names, and every greeting is a kind of prayer for peace.

Each of these men was involved in a conflict when these *Shaloms* happened. Yitro had been an enemy of the Jewish people at one time (according to the midrash). Lavan tried to trick Ya'akov. Yosef's brothers had sold him into slavery. And Boaz had to do a difficult business deal in order to win the right to marry Ruth.

Why were moments of conflict a good time to think about making saying *Shalom* a mitzvah? Here are some lessons about the importance of greeting other people with just a smile (and not even a *Shalom*).

Let people smile at others so that they will be pleased with them.

Rabbeinu Yonah

Even if your heart isn't happy when others arrive, pretend to be happy—let the others think that your face lights up with joy at their coming.

Meiri

Greeting people with a smile is important because it helps you to get control of your anger. Finding a way to smile at a person that you are angry at is a way for you to change you. A smile is the opposite of anger.

Shimon ben Zemah Duran

The Best Jewish Answer: Every book on bullying will tell you that telling the teacher is the correct action. Most kids will tell you that it will do no good. Most of the bullying books will suggest that confronting the bully is a risky intervention that may work, may make things worse, or may make the person who intervenes a new target. In our tests of this material, some of the students suggested that waiting until one is sure that this is bullying and not two friends fooling around is important to do. Each of those three actions may be good, but the best Jewish action is supporting the victim—helping him/her to not feel alone. This is the Jewish value of *someykh noflim*.

Case 3: Ganging Up

Boy's version. A bunk full of boys picks on Jeremy. Robert wants to help Jeremy. **Girl's version.** A bunk full of girls shuns Emma. Ariel wants to help. The potential *rodef shalom* has four choices. Assuming that he or she has learned the lesson of case two and will automatically go and support the victim, the remaining additional choices are: (a) Do nothing; (b) Tell the counselor; (c) Confront the others; (d) Wait and talk to one or two of the kids.

We have already discussed *tokhehah*. In the Bible it is usually translated as "rebuke." That is not an easy word either. *Tokhehah* means telling another person that he or she is doing something wrong. The hard part, as you will learn, is that the mitzvah is to help the other person, not to protect you.

In the Torah we are taught:

> YOU MUST NOT HATE YOUR BROTHER OR SISTER IN YOUR HEART, THEREFORE YOU MUST MAKE SURE TO REBUKE THEM AND NOT BEAR SIN BECAUSE OF THEM.
>
> *Leviticus 19.17*

The Jewish tradition is filled with rules about the best way of doing *tokhehah*. Read each rule. See if you can figure out what is wise about it and what is difficult about it.

> You must not do it in public because you are not allowed to embarrass them when you "correct" them.
>
> *Rashi ad loc.*

> You must rebuke a person who will listen to you. You must not rebuke those that will not listen to you.
>
> *Talmud Bavli, Yevamot 65b*

> If someone is easily embarrassed, you should not just tell him/her that something is wrong. You should begin with conversation about other things. Slowly you can get to talk about the behavior that must change.
>
> *Meor Ha-Tokhehah, p. 11*

> If people you have spoken to about a problem don't change their behavior, you should continue to speak to them as many times as necessary until they change their ways.
>
> *Rambam, Hilkhot Deyot 6.7*

Rabbi Eliyahu Dessler taught, "You cannot criticize someone just to catch him or her at doing something wrong or to prove that you are right. That causes pain and suffering to other people. The Torah forbids this. You are only allowed to give rebuke to a person you want to help. You are only allowed to give rebuke in a positive way."

Mikhtav Me'Eliyahu, vol. 3, p. 139

These texts, many of which we have seen before, define a pattern of intervention. This time, however, it is not an intervention by a teacher, but by of a peer. It is our job to train our students how to give tokhehah in a way that will be heard and accepted. The question in this case is not the how, but the who.

The Best Jewish Answer: As with the previous case, there is potential value or risk in each of the other three—but the best answer is "Talk to one or two of the kids." The research on bullying suggests that there are three types of kids involved in such acts: bullies, bullies' henchmen, and caught-up participants. If you can find those members of the group who are not really part of the gang but who have been caught up by peer pressure, they are the easiest to convince to change their behavior. When you reduce the group and break the crowd you often end the bullying. Therefore, the Jewish value/skill of tokhehah, of learning how to tell another person that he or she is doing something wrong, can be really useful here.

Back to Case 1

When we learn the laws of tokhehah we learn that good feedback can only be given for the sake of the person receiving it, not for our own sake. It can only be given out of caring, not out of anger. Therefore, one sister will need to teach her sister to respect other people's property, but do it for her sake—and not for the sake of protecting her own clothes. That will take a little time to accomplish.

The bottom line is this: Teachers need to know when and how to intervene in bullying by working with the bully. But students need to learn how to intervene in bullying by supporting the victim and by reducing the audience that supports a bully's actions. I once did a workshop on bullying for a group of students in a L.A. suburb and got told a most amazing story. A student said that he and his friends are always on the lookout for kids who are getting picked on. They have a set action. First they invite the student to join them for lunch. Then they interview the "victim" to find out about his interests. Once these are established, they survey their group for another student who shares an interest with the "victim" and then connect the two. This process undoes much of the harm of bullying—that is, the victim's feeling of being alone.

About a month later I retold this story in another synagogue in another L.A. suburb and got told, "We don't dare be seen with the victim, or else we will be picked on." The difference was not a question of geographic location; it was, sadly, an issue of the depth of impact of Jewish values. The answer to bullying ultimately has more to do with what we teach than with what we wind up doing ourselves.

TEACHING WITH STORIES

Hevruta Study

In his important article "Taking Learning Seriously,"
Lee Shulman (1999) wrote, "We now understand that
learning is a dual process in which, initially, the inside
beliefs and understandings must come out, and only then
can something outside get in. To prompt learning, you've
got to begin with the process of going from inside out"
(p. 12). Stories, therefore, are a way to access the learning
that's already inside and then to make connections to larger
themes and patterns. Using stories affirms the value of prior
student experiences both emotionally and cognitively, helps
students make their own meaning, and shows that we take
learners seriously.

Peter Frederick, *The Power of Student Stories: Connections That Enhance Learning*

Stories are more than dramas people tell or read. Story,
as a pattern, is a powerful way of organizing and sharing
individual experience and exploring and co-creating shared
realities. It forms one of the underlying structures of reality,
comprehensible and responsive to those who possess what
we call narrative intelligence. Our psyches and cultures are
filled with narrative fields of influence, or story fields, which
shape the awareness and behavior of the individuals and
collectives associated with them.

Story reality is the reality that we see when we recognize
that every person, every being, every thing has a story

and contains stories and, in fact, is a story—and that all of these stories interconnect, that we are, in fact, surrounded by stories, embedded in stories and made of stories. When poet Muriel Rukeyser tells us "the universe is made of stories, not atoms," she's describing story-reality. Ultimately, story-reality includes any and all actual events and realities, but experience as reality, not as the more usual patterns—objects-and-actions; matter, energy, space, time; patterns of probability; etc. Story-reality is made up of lived stories.

www.co-intelligence.org/I-powerofstory.html

Holy stories are the light of the world. When we understand that, when both tellers and listeners know they are engaged in sacred activity, we will hold stories and storytelling more dear. The teller will tell with the tongue of faith, the listeners will hear with ears of faith, and the circle of holiness will be closed.

Yitzhak Buxbaum, *Storytelling and Spirituality in Judaism*

To care for the soul, it is necessary to shift from causal thinking to an appreciation for story and character, to allow grandparents and uncles to be transformed into figures of myth and to watch certain familiar family stories become canonical through repeated retellings....If we were to observe the soul in the family by honoring its stories and by not running away from its shadow, then we might not feel so inescapably determined by family influences.

Thomas Moore, *Care for the Soul*

The Holy Maggid of Mezritch was an important, world-class Hasidic teacher. He took over from the son of the Baal Shem Tov and became the Rebbe of all Hasidic Jews. But before he was discovered and became a great rebbe, he earned his living as an ordinary Hebrew school teacher in a heder. Later, after he became famous, people became interested in his past. They went to his Hebrew school students and asked them, "What kind of teacher was he?"

One student answered: "He pushed us and pulled us. He asked us questions and he listened to us. He waited until each one of us told him our own story of what it was like to go out of Egypt and cross the Reed Sea. And he waited until each one of us told him our own story of what it was like to stand at Mt. Sinai and accept the Torah."

Retold from Martin Buber, *Tales of the Hasidim*

A person is incapable of a sudden confrontation with the Creator. The overwhelming experience of such awareness is just too awesome. Truth, the stark Truth, must be camouflaged. Only then can the soul gradually absorb it.

God, so to speak, is camouflaged in stories. These are the stories of Creation and of Adam and Eve. The stories of the Flood and of the Patriarchs. The stories of Jewish exile and redemption. God is hidden in all the stories of human history. And in the as-yet-untold stories of each and every human being. His trials. Her tribulations. And their salvation.

At the Pesah seder we tell stories—*maggid*. We recount the stories of the exile in, and the redemption from, Egypt. These represent the collective stories of humankind. They typify the individual stories of each and every one of us. As we relate the details *of* these stories, we must relate *to* them. Be aroused *by* them. See the Hand of God in the stories of our own lives.

Through the *maggid* we bring to life *their* stories. In turn, may God bring to life the story of *our* Redemption.

Nachman of Bretzlav, *Likutey Halakhot, Nedarim* 5:6–8

And when the Mashia<u>h</u> will come, he will also tell stories. The stories of what we all have been through every day of our lives. He will teach the meaning of our past suffering, the redeeming effect of our past tribulations.

Rabbi Nahman's Stories #10, The Burgher and the Pauper, p. 229

Introduction

Ever single article or book on Jewish storytelling includes the following statement:

God created people because God loves stories.

The Midrash

They all also manage to use the following story.

When the great founder of the modern Hasidim, Rabbi Israel Baal Shem Tov, saw misfortune threatening the Jews, it was his custom to go into a certain part of the forest to meditate. There he would light a fire, say a special prayer, and the miracle would be accomplished, and the misfortune or trouble averted.

Later, when his disciple, the celebrated Rabbi Maggid of Mezritch, had occasion, for the same reason, to intercede with heaven, he would go to the same place in the forest and say: "Master of the Universe, listen! I do not know how to light the fire, but I am still able to say the prayer." And again the miracle would be accomplished, disaster was averted, and life continued with its ups and downs.

Still later, Rabbi Moshe-Leib of Sasov, in order to save his people once more (this time, from themselves), would go into the forest and say: "I do not know how to light the fire, I do not know the prayer, but I know the place, and this must be sufficient." It was sufficient, and the miracle of continued life was accomplished.

Then it fell to Rabbi Israel of Rizhyn to overcome misfortune. Sitting in his house, his head in his hands, he spoke to God: "I am unable to light the fire, and I do not know the prayer; I cannot even find the place in the forest. All I can do is to tell the story, and this must be sufficient." And it was sufficient.

Telling from the Rheingold Family Haggadah

I have now touched the necessary dyad.

Teaching with Stories

This is not an article on how to tell stories. Google "storytelling" and you will find pages of articles and sites that will help you grow your skill (or at least they make that assertion). Likewise, this is not a place to list all the Jewish stories you should use. Best source: "Selected and Annotated Bibliography of Current Jewish Story Collections" compiled by Peninnah Schram (www.caje.org/interact/peninah.pdf). You can also Google "Jewish stories" and find enough material to keep you going for years. Our purpose is to talk about what you do with stories, not how you convey them.

Stories can be:

- told well
- told adequately
- played off of a recording
- read out of a book
- read silently by students
- shown from a DVD
- produced as a play, etc.

All of these ways work. So do others. The goal is to communicate a story. This can be done effectively by a teacher who is far from an accomplished storyteller. It is a lot like telling a joke. You can't destroy the punch line, but other than that there are few rules or requirements.

The bigger question is, what do we do once a story is told, read, etc.? The answer is actually simple. We ask one question. It may take a number of questions to get to that one, but essentially we are asking one question: "What lesson do you think this story teaches?"

Back before there was *Understanding by Design* we used to get teachers to write behavioral objectives. In order to write behavioral objectives we used to use a work called *Bloom's Taxonomy of Behavioral Objectives.* The taxonomy breaks learning into six escalating behavioral levels: knowledge, understanding, application, analysis, synthesis, and evaluation. It is believed to be good practice to start by asking "knowledge questions," then "application questions," working one's way up the taxonomy. Our question is an analysis question. The lower-level questions check out the students' understanding of the story and their oral comprehension before we ask an upper-level question. I often skip the lower stages and go straight to the big question, backing up only if I notice a problem. I still feel the need to acknowledge this as good practice.

So let's work with an example. This story is retold from the Midrash.

> This is the story of a king and his son. The king is a father. The son is a prince. One day the prince does something wrong, and he does this thing wrong not for the first time, not for the second time, and not even for the third time. And the father loses his cool. And the father yells at his son, and the son yells back at his father, and this loops for a while, and eventually the son says, "Okay, I'm sorry already." And the father says, "How can I believe you? Because you said you were sorry the first time. And you said you were sorry the second time. And still you did it over and over again." And the son says, "Well, if you don't love me, maybe I shouldn't be here." And the father says, "Well, if you can't behave, maybe you shouldn't be here." And the son says, "I'm leaving." And the father says, "Go." And then he says, "But if you leave, I vow you will never set foot in my house—in this house again."

So the son walks out the door. The one thing we're not told in the Midrash but of which we can be sure is that he slammed the door. The second he's out the door, the king turns to the Secret Service and says, "Follow him. Protect him. Make sure that he's safe, but never, ever let him know that you're there. Never, ever let him know that I cared." The son, meanwhile, has the best time. He goes everywhere he's ever wanted to go. He does everything he's ever wanted to do. There are no "nos" in his life. But this gets old really quickly, and it may be no surprise that the orbit of his perambulations, the distance of his wandering, gets smaller and smaller, and that the son winds up hanging out in the kingdom, quite close to the palace. One day, not by accident but not by plan, father and son meet in the marketplace. And their eyes lock. And they open up their arms, and they run to each other, and they hug each other, and they start to cry, and the dialogue goes, "I love you, I love you, I forgive you, I forgive you," and then the father says the line that makes this whole story worthwhile. He says, "If only I could bring you home again. But I vowed a vow you would never set foot in the house again."

In the next sentence the Midrash gives us our first question. "What should the king do?" There will be lots of suggestions (probably including the "right" answer given in the midrash). There is plenty of time to hear and accept a lot of endings. Only when the discussion is winding down does it make sense to give the ending.

> What did the king do? Since [the palace] was already built, he demolished and rebuilt it and brought his son in. Consequently he permitted him to enter and yet fulfilled his oath.
>
> Retold from *Lamentations Rabbah* 19:20

Now we have two jobs to do. One is to unpack the meaning of the story. The other is to decode its symbolism. First we ask (1) Who is the king? The answer: "In a midrash the king is always God." Then ask: (2) If this is our religion and not another religion talking, who is the son? The answer: "The people of Israel." (3) What is the "palace" in this story? The answer: "The Holy Temple."

Now put it together. What story does this midrash tell? "Why God had the first Temple destroyed and a second Temple built."

This leads us to two final questions that help us unpack the story:

1. What does this story teach about the relationship between God and Israel?

2. What does this story teach about the ways that families work?

So let's understand that this story has at least three different teaching targets: (a) That God had to get some distance from Israel (because of sin) and then decided to start over and rebuild the relationship. (b) That families sometimes go through times of separating and coming back together. When they do this they need to "tear down the palace" and leave the old fights behind and start fresh. (c) That relationships within families are holy, just as the relationship between God and Israel is holy. Holy does not mean smooth all the time. It means with the potential for a special closeness. Therefore question one leads us into theology (and the problem of God needing to start over). Question two leads us into a discussion of families and how they work. It also helps us to put a Jewish spin on the dynamic of family.

If you ask the question "What do you think this story means?" you are likely to get only answers about families. When you unpack the metaphors of God, Israel, and the Temple you enter into a second realm. Stories can teach many things. The questions you choose to ask can deepen (but not limit) the meanings that students derive.

Teaching with Our Own Stories

Teaching with our own stories is an idea I evolved through Hasidic sources but especially via Rabbi Nachman of Bretzlav.

> And when the Mashia<u>h</u> will come, he will also tell stories. The stories of what we all have been through every day of our lives. He will teach the meaning of our past suffering, the redeeming effect of our past tribulations.
>
> *Rabbi Nachman's Stories #10, The Burgher and the Pauper* p. 229

The same idea comes through in the teachings of Levi Yitz<u>h</u>ak of Berditchev.

> The Holy Maggid of Mezritch was an important, world-class <u>H</u>asidic teacher. He took over from the son of the Baal Shem Tov and became the rebbe of all <u>H</u>asidic Jews. But before he was discovered and became a great rebbe he earned his living as a ordinary Hebrew school teacher in a <u>h</u>eder. Later, after he became famous, people became interested in his past. They went to his Hebrew school students and asked them, "What kind of teacher was he?"
>
> One student answered: "He pushed us and pulled us. He asked us questions, and he listened to us. He waited until each one of us told him our own story of what it was like to go out of Egypt and cross the Reed Sea. And he waited until each one of us told him our own story of what it was like to stand at Mt. Sinai and accept the Torah."
>
> *Tales of the Hasidim*

For about ten years I have turned these shared insights into a workshop I call "It Only Takes Four Stories to Be Jewish." Here are the four stories.

1. God created the world, and I was one of God's creations.

2. I was a slave in Egypt, and God took me out.

3. I stood at Sinai, and I heard God teach Torah.

4. God will redeem the world, and I am part of that redemption.

What I do is to invite individuals or groups to share their most important family stories. Then I explain to them which of the four categories their story fits into. It becomes an exciting process that grows as people hear some of the other stories and grow the number of stories they can tell. Stories build on stories. Here are a few examples of stories I have transcribed.

- My grandmother was Orthodox. She was a master baker. She baked for every *simhah*. She also had heart disease, and my mother never forgave her for not remembering the law that you shouldn't risk your life to perform a mitzvah. She continued to bake and risk her health. My mother never forgave her, and because of that she never passed her recipes on to me. A few years ago I went on a synagogue retreat. I got a *hallah* recipe from *The Jewish Catalog* and made *hallah* for the first time in my life. Since then I have been changing and changing the recipe. I am convinced that I have recreated the taste of my grandmother's *hallah* even though I never tasted it.

- I grew up a liberal white child in a Southern town. My mother was Jewish; my father owned the newspaper. Once we stopped for gas, and the person who came out to serve the gas started to say all these bigoted things—things against Jews. My mother sat quietly. I sat quietly, but my brother Phil's blood boiled. He said, "You'd better watch what you say, because my mother is Jewish." That quieted the attendant. My mother then told my brother, "Hey, that makes you Jewish, too." The big surprise in my life was that I turned out Jewish when no one else did. Because my mother was Jewish, I was Jewish, too.

- I was diagnosed with a terminal disease. I was really depressed. I basically stopped living. One afternoon I went out onto my porch and started eating chocolate chip cookies. The flavor of the cookies overwhelmed me. They were delicious. I just ate and ate. This was my sunrise. I realized that I wanted to take in as many wonderful and sweet things as I could. Starting that afternoon, I decided to live as long as I could and fill my life with as much as I can.

- My Nana Rose lived in Kishnev under Czarist rule. One year Passover and Easter overlapped, and there were two days worth of pogroms. My nana survived the pogrom hidden in a haystack, made it to New York, but later died on an abortionist's table. Fifteen years after she died, I am in a hospital bed, really angry with God. A rabbi comes to see me. He suggests to me an old Jewish custom, the changing of my name. He gives me a new Hebrew name, Shoshana (Rose). He picked the name without knowing my family story. It has given me a lot of strength.

- An Orthodox feminist proudly tells this story. "My grandfather was the rabbi of a small town in Eastern Europe. My grandmother was the rebbetzin. Every Friday night she set a large table for the family and for many guests. After the table was set she would go into her room to change. As soon as she was gone, my grandfather would run in, steal one of the two _hallot_ (loaves of Shabbat bread) off the table, and run and take it to a poor family who would otherwise have no Shabbat. As soon as he was out the door, my grandmother would reenter the dining room, steal the other _hallah,_ and run off and take it to another needy family. Later, when they sat down at the Shabbat table, the _hallah_ cover was now covering an empty plate. Each of them ignored that obvious reality for a while. When it came time to bless the bread, my grandfather would tap the table and ask, '_Nu,_ woman, where is the _hallah_?' She would answer, 'Old man, you are not going to heaven by yourself, you are not the only one who will have a place in the _olam ha-ba_ (the world to come).'"

- My mother's grandparents left Germany and went to Spain. From Spain they went to Cuba to escape the Holocaust. They worked really hard. Grandma was a baker, and Grandpa delivered the baked goods. They worked day and night and lived with cockroaches. It was not an easy life. When Rosh ha-Shanah came they went to work; they felt that they had little choice. When they came home from a long day at work they found a surprise—their neighbors had made a Rosh ha-Shanah dinner. Their table was set, and food was on the table. The biggest surprise was the suckling pig with the apple in its mouth that was sitting in the middle of the table.

- My brother went to school in Flagstaff. My mother flew out to meet him. He met her at the plane with a borrowed pickup truck. She was all dressed up in a Dior suit, expensive name-brand shoes and the like. They began the couple-of-hours' drive up through the mountains. About halfway, he pulled the truck over and said, "We are camping for the night." My mother worked hard to control her temper and said little. They ate, and she was given a sleeping bag to use in the back of the pickup. She had a pretty restless night. My brother slept on the ground. When the sun came up the next morning she realized that the truck had been backed to the edge of a cliff, and she could look out of the tailgate, across the high desert plateau, and directly at the sunrise coming up over the mountains. It took her breath away. It was a moment of pure awe. She then understood why her son had moved halfway across the country to the end of the earth.

Here is your homework assignment: Match each of the stories found above with one of the four categories of stories found at the top of this section.

My friend Rabbi Ed Feinstein does a similar kind of thing with sunrise and sunset stories. He has people tell them and then sings their story back to them in the *nusah* (melody) of the service. He then adds in Hebrew and English *Barukh atah adonai yotzer ha-meorot*—Praised are you, Eternal, the one who creates lights. That is the morning formula. In the evening he substitutes the evening formula. He builds a prayer out of people's stories. Another friend, Rabbi Phil Warmflash, took the idea and now says, "Tell me the story of your Exodus." He then connects those stories to the second blessing before the Shema, which has an Exodus theme.

You can do the same thing for most topics. Imagine you want to do a lesson on the *kippah*; start with stories about "the most important hat in your house (and why it is important)." Name the topic, and you can figure out the chance for your students (and their families) to tell their own stories.

The big deal here is the idea that every family story is a Jewish story. The Bible is true, not because it happened back then, but because it happened and re-happens as part of our own family history. What is ancient is also modern and part of our lives!

TEACHING FOR FRIENDSHIP— *KONEI LEKHA HAVER*

Hevruta Study

Joshua ben Perahyah said: "To live a good life you need to do three things: (1) find a teacher, (2) make a friend (*konei lekha haver*), and (3) give everyone else the benefit of the doubt."

Pirkei Avot 1.6

A friend is someone you eat and drink with.
A friend is someone with whom you study Torah (God's word)
and with whom you study Mishnah (ethics and laws).
A friend is someone who sleeps over
or at whose house you can spend the night.
Friends teach each other secrets,
the secrets of the Torah
and secrets of the real world, too.

Avot d'Rabbi Natan

Never stop trying to make more friends. At the same time, having even one enemy is too many.

Orhot Hayyim of the Rosh no. 90

In *Pirkei Avot* it says "*Konei lekha haver,*" "Be willing to pay to have a friend." It will cost you to have a friend. You may have to spend money. You may have to spend time and energy to keep a friend. You may have to put up with some bad habits that your friend has. You will probably even wind up in quarrels with your friend. But having a close friend is worth all of the effort.

Ralbag, Ha'Deyot v'ha Midot 14.3

Nothing helps you work as hard as having a friend who is trying to succeed at the same goal. When we work alone we can make mistakes and fool ourselves. When we talk things over with a friend we can correct each other's thinking, and we can help each other find new ideas, too.

Wisdom of Mishle, p. 183

A person cannot be at his or her best without a friend with whom to talk things over and who will offer advice. The Talmud says "Either a friend or death" *(Bava Batra 16b)*. A person without a friend is like a left hand without a right one.

Sefer ha-Midot leha-Meiri

Let the honor of your friend be as dear to you as your own.

Pirkei Avot 2.15

Let the property of your friend be as precious to you as your own.

Pirkei Avot 2.17

On the day of your friend's success, participate in her joy.

Ecclesiastes Rabbah 7.22

One who becomes elevated at the expense of a friend's shame has no share in the World to Come.

Jerusalem Talmud, Hagigah 2.1

A person who tries to keep everything personal hidden will not have close friends. Building relationships with others requires self-disclosure.

Rabbi Yitzhak Hunter, Pahad Yitzhak: Iggerot u'K'tuvim, p. 236

This chapter has three distinct purposes. First, we are interested in understanding why the building of friendship is a concern for Jewish teachers. Second, we want to establish that there are Jewish things to teach that expand the understanding of friendship. Third, we want to examine class procedures and techniques that enhance the development of friendships. But most of all, we want our students' friendships to become a topic of concern.

For Want of a Friend

There is a childhood nursery rhyme:

> For want of a nail the shoe was lost.
> For want of a shoe the horse was lost.
> For want of a horse the rider was lost.
> For want of a rider the battle was lost.
> For want of a battle the kingdom was lost.
> And all for the want of a horseshoe nail.

This poem has a huge amount to teach us about the Jewish future. Let's start with a simple question (that I usually ask parents). "What is the best way to get an 11- to 15-year-old child to go to services?" The number one answer is usually "a good hammerlock." The right answer is "Let them meet and sit with a friend." The same answer is the best answer for "How do you get a Jewish kid to go to youth group?" "attend a Jewish camp?" "participate in an Israel program?" and (the million-dollar question) "continue with Jewish education past bar or bat mitzvah?" For want of a friend the Jewish battle can be lost. Because friends get kids into Jewish communities, and Jewish communities get them to continue Jewish life once they have left home and to seek other Jewish communities once they have grown up.

If our Jewish teaching is concerned with building the Jewish future, then Hebrew school friendships are as much part of our construction as are *brakhot* (blessings), Hebrew reading, and knowledge of the Jewish holidays. Perhaps more!

Teachers often feel friendships are our enemies. Friendships invite note passing, talking, laughing, texting, pranks, and a lot more. Friendships get in the way of our absolute demand for focus from each student and our need for total control. Get over it. Understand that if your classroom only builds good Hebrew school and day school friendships, *dayenu*!

Toward a Friendship Curriculum

Read this story.

> Moshe Lev of Sasov said that he learned about being a friend by listening to two drunk Russian peasants in a tavern. The first said, "Ivan, do you love me?" Ivan said, "Of course I love you, friend. You are closer to me than my own brother." The first then asked, "Do you love me more than you love you?" Ivan answered, "Absolutely." Then the first peasant said, "Ivan, if you love me so much, how come you didn't notice that I cut my hand and that blood is gushing out?" Moshe Lev used to explain, "From him I learned that to be a good friend is to feel a friend's pain."
>
> Adapted from Martin Buber, *Tales of the Hasidim*

Here is a beautiful Jewish insight into friendship. To be a good friend one must know when a friend is in pain. We have a lot of friendships that are built on having fun, and that is okay, but to deepen a friendship we have to be there in harder, more difficult times. Nice lesson.

Here are three more friendship texts that reveal some more insights.

JUST AS FACE ANSWERS FACE IN A REFLECTION IN WATER, SO SHOULD ONE PERSON'S HEART ANSWER ANOTHER *(Proverbs 27:19)*. This verse teaches a principle that is important in our relationships with others. We all want others to be friendly and kind to us, but we can't directly control their behavior. We can only control our own behavior. We play a large role in creating the world we live in, especially how others will behave toward us. If you behave toward others in a positive manner, they are likely to reciprocate. When you act aggressively and with hostility toward others, they are likely to behave in a similar manner toward you. When you shout at people, they are likely to shout back at you. On the other hand, if you are caring and cheerful toward others, they are apt to feel love for you. Purely for pragmatic reasons we should be kind and friendly in dealing with others.

Rabbi Zelig Pliskin, *Gateway to Happiness*, p. 136

I loved the verse from Proverbs in this quote so much that it is now the signature on all my e-mail. It is Martin Buber's idea of "I and Thou" wrapped up in a single verse. Rabbi Zelig Pliskin is the author of more than twenty books, including *Guard Your Tongue, Love Thy Neighbor, Gateway to Happiness*, and *Building Your Self-Image and the Self-Image of Others*. He is a master at collecting Jewish sources and one of the inspirations for this book. Here he teaches that friendship is built out of behavior. Certain kinds of behavor make and grow friendships.

The following two texts were culled from Rabbi Pliskin's book *Love Thy Neighbor.*

Every person you meet deeply desires to be treated with respect. If you listen carefully, you will hear their cry: "Please consider me an important person." "Don't embarrass or insult me." "Please listen to me when I speak." *(Rabbi Yeruchem Levovitz, Da'at Hokhmah u'Mussar, vol. 3, p. 68)*

Here is a wonder, a simple truth. Everyone is lonely. Everyone is needy. Everyone is searching for friends, for people with whom they can connect.

> A person who tries to keep everything personal hidden will not have close friends. Building relationships with others requires self-disclosure.
>
> Rabbi Yitzhak Hunter, *Pahad Yitzhak: Iggerot u'K'tuvim*, p. 236

Again, a simple truth: Friendship requires risk. One must share things with a friend in order to cement the friendship.

Finally one last text, one you've seen before in this book:

> A friend is someone you eat and drink with.
> A friend is someone with whom you study Torah (God's word)
> and with whom you study Mishnah (ethics and laws).
> A friend is someone who sleeps over
> or at whose house you can spend the night.
> Friends teach each other secrets,
> the secrets of the Torah
> and secrets of the real world, too.
>
> *Avot d'Rabbi Natan*

Here is the ultimate Jewish school text. The central idea is profound: Friendships build learning, and learning builds friendship. This is the foundation of building a Jewish school rooted in friendships.

The Pedagogy of Friendship

Here are some pieces from my friend Carol Starin on ways of teaching that build friendships.

Students have friends. This is particularly important in supplementary schools. Our students come from many neighborhoods. Many of our students don't know each other.

Hebrew school is sometimes a very lonely place for kids. It's hard to be joyous when you are lonely. Every time you plan something, ask yourself, How can I help students get to know each other?

Here is a list of suggestions for creating situations in which kids must learn and talk together.

- Design lunch, recess, and transition activities that "force" kids to talk to each other.
- Design your classroom in ways that encourage group work, cooperative learning groups, study in _hevruta._
- Create a mitzvah project everyone works on together.
- Institute a buddy system in which kids must call each other to find out about homework and to collaborate on a project.
- If appropriate, extend the learning to e-mail discussions.
- Structure learning that promotes interaction, encourages cooperative work, and empowers students to learn from and with each other.
- Use peer teaching.

Five Ways to Build Community in the Classroom

What does a classroom community look like? It looks like students asking each other for help and information. It looks like students taking responsibility for themselves and for each other. It looks like students working together and learning with and from each other. The words you use, the learning strategies you create and the ways you structure activities can foster that kind of community. How does a group of kids in a Jewish classroom become a _kehillah_ (community)? Here are five ways to begin building community in your classroom. These ideas are not one-time games or "getting to know you" activities, but strategies that help children get to know each other in meaningful ways that promote collaboration and shared responsibility.

1. **Build self-esteem.** Each week one student is invited to experience "fifteen minutes of fame." Students sit in a circle, and each student says one positive thing about the day's chosen student. Suggested opening sentences: "I really like you because…." "Thank you for the time that you…." My favorite thing about you is…." This exercise works with any age group but can't begin until students have "lived together" for a few weeks. And it's a good activity for building self-esteem. Be sure you plan the timing so that over the course of a school year every student gets his/her "fifteen minutes of fame."

2. **Create a Class Directory.** Develop a roster that lists contact information for everyone in the class, including families, teacher, *madrikhim*, and information about the school. Remember to include contact information for all the primary care givers (some students live in more than one place). Also, remember to include space for new students who join the class later in the year, as well as space for students to make notes. Create the directory as a class project so kids can take ownership in the process. Once the directory is complete, give students homework they have to do on the phone. The goal is to create situations that foster and nurture friendships. An example: Every student is assigned a buddy. When Michael is absent he receives a call from his buddy to fill him in on the classwork and go over the homework assignment.

3. **Use inclusive language.** Use "our" instead of "my". Be vigilant about giving the message that the classroom and everything in it belong to everyone. Use "our classroom, our homework, our *tzedakah* project, our *siddurim*."

4. **Empower students to use each other as resources.** From Carol Cummings *(Managing To Teach, 1984)* I learned this trick: "Ask three before me." What page are we on? How do you spell

Hanukkah? Where are the glue sticks? Instead of hands waving in the air to ask the teacher, encourage students to turn to each other by enforcing the "ask three before me" rule. During group work, center time, and seat work, students who have a question must ask another student for the answer (up to three other students) before asking the teacher.

5. **Plan for learning strategies that encourage collaboration.**

- Learning in pairs, _hevruta_, is an authentically Jewish way to study. Create independent study activities that students need to do in groups of two.

- Use learning centers as opportunities for students to work together informally. Example: After class reading and discussion about Hanukkah, students are invited to do follow-up projects at centers. At one center students must share crayons, markers, and other materials for coloring a _hanukkiyah_. At another, students work together to write a Hanukkah verse to the class holiday song.

- Try the "think, pair, share" strategy. First ask a question that everyone needs to think about. Next, ask students to turn to their neighbors to share the thinking. Then ask each pair to share their thinking with the entire class.

Putting Friendship into Practice

We've explored the hows and whys of building friendship in the classroom. If you want to change the world, one simple way is by putting this chapter into practice. Just as you can easily change the feel of your classroom by putting the greeting and respect units into practice, you can most change how kids report about your teaching if you help them to make and reinforce friendships. Make this an important part of your job.

TEACHING VALUES

Hevruta Study

A medieval book called the *Orhot Tzadikkim* suggests reciting this creed regularly. It is a listing of all the behaviors that come from the mitzvah of "You shall love your neighbor as yourself" (Leviticus 19.18). We have already learned that teaching is an expression of this mitzvah.

- I should help others in every way possible according to my ability.
- I should trouble myself for rich and poor alike.
- I should lend money to anyone who needs a loan (at no interest).
- I should give presents to the poor according to my ability and, from time to time, send presents to the wealthy also.
- If I have business dealings with others, I must be entirely honest.
- I must not be strict with others in small matters.
- I wish always to give pleasure to others, and not vice versa, to speak pleasantly to everyone.
- If someone deceives me, I will not deceive him/her back.
- I will bear the yoke of others but will not cause others trouble.
- I will not quarrel.
- I will greet every person with joy and a pleasant facial expression, for this will strengthen love.
- I will deal with others for their good.
- When others are sad and worried, I will comfort them.

- If persons confide their secrets to me, I will not reveal them to others even if they anger me.
- I will not speak evil of others and will not listen to others speak evil.
- I will always try to find some merit in others.
- I should honor every person with deeds and with words.
- I should not act condescendingly toward anyone.

Orhot Tzadikim, The Gate of Love

When I share this list with teachers, some of these items seem really problematic to them. Among them are: (a) I should lend money to anyone who needs a loan (at no interest). This one seems to violate the distance that teachers feel they need from their students. Interesting! (b) I will bear the yoke of others but will not cause others trouble. This one seems to some teachers (and parents) to create a masochistic personality and violate the premise of even sharing. And (c) I should give presents to the poor according to my ability and, from time to time, send presents to the wealthy also. The mention of economic status seems to some to be a no-no. All three of these—in fact, all of the items on the list—have good presence in the Talmud and represent key Torah values. It is perfectly okay that these (or others) make you uncomfortable. You might want to use your discomfort as an opportunity to do some more learning.

1. The general rule is that anything you would want others to do for you, you should do for others.
2. You must visit someone who is ill.
3. You must comfort someone who is mourning.
4. You must help people to get married.
5. You must help a bride and groom rejoice at their wedding.
6. You must be hospitable to guests.
7. You must attend someone's funeral and help in any way during the burial.

8. You must give constructive criticism to someone who does something that others think is odd.

9. You must lend money or any other article to someone in need.

10. You must pray for someone's well-being.

11. A craftsman must make his product for the benefit of the person who will use it, and not just as a source of income.

12. You must forgive others for wronging you.

13. You must teach others Torah.

14. A doctor must heal people.

15. You must greet others with a cheerful face.

16. You must give someone change for their larger coin or bill.

17. You must run to tell someone good news.

18. You must supply others with kosher food if they cannot get it themselves.

19. You must protect others from injury.

20. You must share the feelings of sorrow and suffering of others.

21. You must feel happiness for others' good fortune.

22. You must warn others about possible loss or damage.

23. You must pick up someone's garment if you see it lying on the floor.

24. You must give others helpful advice whenever possible.

25. You must cheer someone up when you see that he is sad or lonely.

26. You must write letters to your relatives in other cities so that they do not worry about you.

27. You must return books to their proper place in a library, synagogue, or yeshiva so that others will be able to find them.

28. You may not rejoice at the misfortunes of others.

29. You may not unnecessarily make noise that would disturb the sleep of others.

30. You are forbidden to curse others.

31. You are forbidden to cause someone pain or unpleasantness through your actions or words.

32. If you see someone suffering, you must save him from further suffering. In addition, even before a person suffers, if you are able to save him from future suffering, you are obligated to do so.

33. You must not be jealous of the good fortune of others.

34. You must not speak *lashon ha-ra* about others, for no one wants others to speak *lashon ha-ra* about him.

35. You must always judge others favorably.

36. You must not keep people waiting.

37. You must try to save others from needless exertion.

38. You must do all you can to give others pleasure.

39. You should be very careful not to become angry with others.

40. Parents must love others as their own children. The same applies to one's spouse's children and brothers and sisters. It is necessary to mention, since some people are careful to do *hesed* for strangers but forget that they have a similar, and even greater, obligation toward their relatives.

And

41. Consult a *halakhic* authority when you have a question about your obligation to help others to which you do not know the answer.

Sridai Aish, vol.5 4, p. 343

Mensch

Mensch is a Yiddish word for "maximum human being." In English we say, "What do you expect? I'm only human." In the Jewish tradition we say, "Be a *mensch*." Rather than seeing "human" as a limitation, we see it as a source of potential.

This book is not designed to be a child obedience manual. It is not intended to get your children to cave in to your will, because it has a much higher goal, and that is to get each student to take responsibility for becoming a kind, caring, empathic, responsible person who is always working on becoming even better. Once you've done that, your job is pretty much over. You can turn in your keys and give up your job as the parole officer and the prison warden. You can stop worrying about controlling and limiting every aspect of your students' behavior. Instead you can take up your position as friend and coach as they take responsible control of the people they are becoming.

The first secret of this book is that in order to lead your children on the journey, you will have to go on your own parallel journey.

More Than Following Rules

A *mensch* needs to do a lot more than follow rules. The Talmud explains it with a story.

> In Talmudic times rabbi was not a job, it was something that people did after work. Rabbis did not take money for teaching Torah, for helping people solve problems using Torah, or for helping a person find inner peace. Rabbi Shimon ben Shetah was the best teacher in Jerusalem, and he was old and poor. During the day, to earn his living, he sold cloth door to door, and then he

taught hundreds of students at night. His students knew that he would not take money for his teaching, so they decided to buy him a gift. The chipped in and bought him a donkey. They got the donkey from a non–Jewish vendor, and to make sure that the deal was clear, they repeated to him the Jewish first rule of acquisition. "We give you the money. You give to us the reins to the donkey. When we pull on the reins and the donkey takes a step, the donkey, the saddle, the blanket, the bridle, and even the fleas on the donkey are ours." When they gave the donkey to their rabbi and showed him how to take care of it, a ruby fell out from between the saddle and the blanket. Rabbi Shimon ben Sheta_h_ told his students to return the ruby to the vendor. They told the rabbi, "Because we were clear about how we made the deal, the law says that the ruby is yours." The rabbi said, "The law is one thing, but *derekh eretz*, the right thing to do, says that you have to return it." When they returned to the vendor he was tearing his business apart, hunting for the ruby. When they returned it he made it clear that he knew the law and that it was theirs. When they still gave it back, he fell down on his knees and said, "God bless the God of Rabbi Shimon ben Sheta_h_."

Yerushalmi Bava Metzia, 2. 8c; Deuteronomy Rabbah 3.5

This book is about helping your students develop both the heart and the will to return the ruby.

Four Tools

When you cull the Jewish tradition you find that four tools speak directly to parents, giving them ways to raise their children. We are going to work with these four tools.

Step One: Defining Values and Deep-Rooting Them with Stories and Quotations

It is very hard to hit a target if you don't know where it is. Teachers' first responsibility is to "hang a target" and make it clear that hitting it is the goal.

Think of it this way. When marine trainers want to teach porpoises to do tricks, they do it with rewards and not words. In the beginning, when the animals do something that might come close to starting the trick, they get fish. Slowly the conditions for rewards become more exacting, and eventually the porpoises come to master the given behavior. The process is slow and the behaviors limited, because words aren't involved.

With people it is possible to "purpose" and not "porpoise." We can use words and images, and we can give feedback, making learning easier and faster and making harder tricks possible.

The Jewish tradition has long since figured out that naming values makes them easier to live. In the same way that the Eskimos have oodles of words for snow, we have a special language of behavior, because that is an arena of great concern to us (as important a part of our daily lives as snow is to an Eskimo).

Starting in the Bible, Jews figured out that stories are the best way to convey a value. (And we have already talked about teaching with stories.) Stories are slices of life—they come as close to personal experience as we can get without actually having that experience. And they become reference points, yardsticks that help us make sense out of our experiences.

William Bennett has already widely popularized this approach in his *Book of Virtues* and subsequent work. He knows this old Jewish truth, but the Jewish tradition also knew that knowing about "the right" was not enough. People struggling to be good faced two problems. The first was what to do when two values we believe in strongly conflict. The second was what to do when "what I know is right" conflicts with "what I really want." (If this latter problem were easy, people would only have to diet once in their lives—the first diet would work, and that would be the end.) The next couple of steps work on those issues.

Step Two: You Be the Judge—Rehearsing Value Conflicts

The Torah does not spend a lot of time stating values; instead it gives situations. It doesn't say "Be responsible for your animals." Instead it says "When an ox gores..." and gives three cases: (a) another ox, (b) another ox for the second time, or (c) a person. The three situations call for three different responses. In the Talmud we literally have almost a whole book of "goring ox" cases. This is not because the Jewish tradition was big on situation ethics, but rather because we believe that as the balance of values changes, the response has to change. When one ox gores another, we only know which ox won, not who started the fight. A very peaceful ox could have had a very good parry and riposte. However, once an ox has been blooded, the responsibility of the owner changes. Once an ox has shown itself capable of causing damage, the moral need to guard that ox is greater. The second time that ox hurts another animal, the owner is clearly at fault (because there already was a warning), and that ox is now clearly a danger. The intensity of obligation increases further if a person and not another animal is involved, because human life is more valuable, and that already-possibly-dangerous animal was somehow allowed access to people.

So what does this discussion of goring oxen have to do with teaching children? What we learn is the value of "rehearsals." This lesson comes in a few parts.

First, the "right thing to do" involves analysis of a situation and not simply one value in action. As an ox owner, I do not want to spend huge amounts of money guarding each and every ox. So I need to ask myself what is reasonable ox guarding. I have the need to protect people and other animals on one hand, and the need to make a reasonable profit on the other. What I choose to do, what my guarding practice is, should be a responsible balance. That balance changes when an ox becomes known to be more dangerous. By studying these ox rules I also learn about taking care of dogs, gerbils (which are illegal in California because of the damage they can cause crops), etc. Through these case studies we develop a way of thinking about problems.

Second, it can prevent problems. By worrying about how much I will have to pay if my ox hurts another ox (or a person), I begin to think more clearly about the conditions for taking care of my ox, my dog, my hamster, and my son's three pet snakes.

Third, we begin to store solutions that we can use later. We usually have to make our worst ethical decisions under great pressure, when we are under emotional overload. There is a lot of screaming inside our brain. To use an extreme example, living wills are great rehearsals. If we have to decide whether to treat an elderly relative or let him or her die, the pressure is amazing. If we have already had that conversation, if we know what we believe and what the relative wants, facing that choice is much easier. The same is true of lesser and less significant issues.

Finally, these case studies create fun arguments that (a) allow children to explore their values and their consequences, and (b) allow teachers to share their value systems without needing to impose them.

This kind of case study–centered teaching has been popularized in the *Moral Development* work of Robert Kohlberg and his school and in the *Values Clarification* work of Sidney Simon and the rest of his crew.

A living Mishnah story makes this point. A few years ago I was teaching Mishnah to a seventh grade class. We started the year with a passage that teaches what to do if two people both claim to have found the same thing—in this case, a coat. The Mishnah instructs the judges to have each claimant take the following oath: "I swear to God that no less than half this coat is mine." The reason for the "no less than half" formula is rooted in the fact that Jews obsess over being absolutely true whenever they invoke God's name. Six months go by. I make the mistake of letting both Brett and Ben go to the bathroom at the same time. Suddenly the door flies open. Ben is standing there. He informs the class that Brett threw him down, broke his arm, and urinated over the bathroom floor. Brett then hurled Ben into the room with this counter claim: "Ben was the one who urinated all over the bathroom floor." While the two boys stand there screaming at each other, throwing the blame one to the other, I am in the front completely thrown, totally unsure what to do. Kent comes to my rescue when he raises his hand and says, "We'll solve it the Mishnah way. Each of them has to take an oath that no less than half the urine on the bathroom floor is his." It is brilliant. Kent has taken a case we studied about shared ownership of acquired property and applied it to sharing responsibility for a misdeed. That is the way ethical rehearsals work. The more solutions you've worked through in advance, the more you can respond instantaneously.

Step Three: A Self-Healing, Self-Correcting Discipline System

Jim Fay is a teacher educator we will quote regularly in the course of this work. He runs the Love & Logic Institute in Denver. One of his core ideas is profoundly Jewish: "We want our students to make mistakes, lots of mistakes, when the consequences are affordable."

The Jewish version of this idea is *t'shuvah*, repentance. It is a system that teaches people to take responsibility for their actions by (1) admitting when they are wrong, (2) offering apologies where appropriate, (3) fixing whatever was broken (including feelings), and (4) doing the inner work so that when the same buttons are pushed the reaction will be different the next time. (We have already talked about *t'shuvah* as a part of classroom management.)

Our goal here is to slowly transfer both control and responsibility for behavior from us to our students. We want to hold them accountable for their actions—and that includes fixing their own mistakes. While not letting them get away with more than we would under any other system, our job here is to stop punishing and start coaching.

Lawrence Kohlberg developed a theory of moral development. He postulated that people grow through six states of maturity in their ethical problem solving. His lowest stage is the State of Punishment and Obedience: I do not do "bad things" because I am afraid of getting caught and punished. His highest stage is the Stage of Universal Ethical Principles. This is a commitment to act in behalf of things just because they are right—cosmically correct. Kohlberg believed that few people—only people like Gandhi—reached this final stage. In between a person's motivation for doing good changes to (a) it affects people I care about, then (b) it is the rule, and then (c) it is what society needs.

One way of looking at Kohlberg's system is not in terms of the kind of the logic used by individuals (his primary focus), but in terms of a perception of who gets hurt. We start out doing or not doing things based on "me." Then we worry about "people who are close to me." Finally we move outward to "my community," and then later "global concern."

If Kohlberg is right—and besides the research data, there is a lot of good Jewish thought that matches his thinking—we need to help our students learn who is hurt or who is helped by each of their actions. We learn about hurt not when we are punished, but when we have to take responsibility for our actions—when we have to work to fix the hurt. That is the purpose of this third step. Through coaching and the constant transfer of responsibility we want to help our children be aware of the hurt they cause and the healing and help they can effect.

Step Four: Being a Role Model

Most of us would start with being a role model as number one. We make it number four, because it is actually the hardest of the steps. The problem is that children readily read our hypocrisy, and our worst actions frequently undermine our best. We will say much about this later. Let us simply say here that the best example you can set for your children is being wrong when you are wrong. Accepting the responsibility for being wrong is a powerful gift because it gives your children permission to be wrong and work on their weaknesses, too.

Here's What *Menschlekeit* Looks Like

Here are some classical Jewish examples of what *menschlekeit* looks like.

Repentence (*T'shuvah*): You leave your students alone in the room for a moment. They wind up breaking a vase with a football. As soon as you walk in the door a student leader says, "We were messing around in a way we shouldn't have been. We broke the vase. We are sorry. We figured it out, and it should take us about four weeks to buy you a new one. I am sorry that we didn't live up to the responsibility you put in our hands. We think I know how to do better next time." (And you believe all of this is sincere—because it is.)

Forgiveness (*Slihah*): Your two sisters get in a fight. The oldest uses her "better tools" and makes her sister cry. Later she comes in and says she is sorry, but the younger sister says, "Go away. You hurt me." The older sister waits a bit, then tries again. This time the younger sister says, "Now I am ready. Let's start again."

Rebuke (*Tokhehah*): You go to a child who never passes things in on time and say, "Getting your report finished is your responsibility, but I am worried that you are not far enough along at this point." He swallows deeply, resists yelling at you, and says, "You're right, it is my responsibility, but thanks for the hint. I am getting behind." (And he does put in more time—even beyond when you are watching.)

Loving Your Neighbor (*V'ahavta l'Reyekha K'mokhah*): A student walks back to the snack area to return ten dollars in extra change that the volunteer behind the table gave her when she bought a juice. She discovered it only when she recounted her money to plan for tomorrow. When you ask "Why?" she answers, "I don't want the money not to go to the homeless shelter we are funding."

Controlling Anger (*Erekh Apayim*): An old student comes to your room. He mumbles something about how his teacher cheated him and was unfair. You say something like "What happened?" But he says nothing. He sits silently at first with his fists clenched. Then he says, "Now I am ready to talk about it calmly."

The Right Way (*Derekh Eretz*): A student finds a necklace in a box in a bag on the bus. She takes the bag back to the store, goes to the help desk, and gets them to trace the receipt and contact the person who lost it. She spends more than an hour returning a piece of jewelry that was worth less than twenty dollars.

Groundless Hate (*Sinat Hinam*): Your son asks to borrow a friend's computer game. The friend refuses to share. A few weeks later, the friend asks your son to borrow one of his videotapes. Rather than holding a grudge, he says, "Sure."

Being a Friend (*Hevruta*): During class you catch a twelve-year-old texting her best friend. She turns to you and says, "Dale broke up with Roger, and she needs me." You smile, point at your watch, and head back to teaching as she texts one final message and closes her cell phone.

Pursuing Peace (*Rodef Shalom*): Two friends are fighting. Something stupid happened at a party, and now they are feuding and trying to get one of your students to choose one of them. Your student goes into mediator mode, doing shuttle diplomacy, and brings the two friends back together.

Preventing Shame (*Bushah*): During recess David missed the final foul shot and missed the chance of tying the big game. The whole school except for two of your students starts using the sarcastic nickname "Clutch." Even though they were not particularly friendly with him, your two students now make a point of using "Dave" in front of everyone and of spending extra time with him.

Taking Care of Your Body (*Shmirat ha-Guf*): When you teach about sex, smoking, and drugs with your students, you know you can relax because they regularly tell you, "My body is a gift from God. I've got an obligation to take care of it." You believe them, because they are regularly living out this commitment.

Guarding One's Tongue (*Shmirat ha-Lashon*): A girl comes to class in a pretty hideous outfit. You know that the rest of the girls hate it and think it looks silly, but as soon as she shows it off, before she even asks, you smile and say, "You look really proud of that choice. It's great that you got something you really like."

BIBLIOGRAPHY

Jewish Values, Jewish Virtues

Teaching Jewish Virtues, Susan Friedman, Alternatives in Religious Education

The Jewish Moral Virtues, Eugene B. Borowitz, Frances Weinman Schwartz, Jewish Publication Society

Love Your Neighbor, Zelig Pliskin, Aish ha-Torah Press

Jewish Values from Alef to Tav, Joel Lurie Grishaver, Torah Aura Productions

Content of Their Character Instant Lesson: Erekh Apayim, Joel Lurie Grishaver, Torah Aura Productions

Content of Their Character Instant Lesson: T'shuvah, Joel Lurie Grishaver, Torah Aura Productions

Content of Their Character Instant Lesson: V'ahavta Re'ekha K'mokha, Joel Lurie Grishaver, Torah Aura Productions

Using Halakhic Cases to Rehearse the Application of Values

*How Good People Make Tough Choices, Rushworth M. Kidder, William Morrow and Co.

*Mah La'asot, Janice Alper, Torah Aura Productions

*Jewish Law Review Vol. 1, Morley Feinstein, Torah Aura Productions

*Jewish Law Review Vol. 2, Hillel Gameron, Torah Aura Productions

*Rabbinic Driving Manual, David Meyer, Torah Aura Productions

*You Be the Judge, Case Load One, Joel Lurie Grishaver, Torah Aura Productions

*You Be the Judge, Case Load Two, Nahum Amsel, Torah Aura
   Productions

*You Be the Judge, Case Load Three, Joel Lurie Grishaver, Torah Aura
   Productions

Judge for Yourself Courtroom Drama Game, Pressman

What's Right, What's Wrong: A Guide to Talking About Values for
   Parents and Kids by Jeff Marx and Risa Munitz Gruberger, Reader's
   Digest

Creating a Self-Healing Environment

*Teaching with Love and Logic/Parenting with Love and Logic, Jim Fay
   & David Funk, Love & Logic Press

*Four Steps to Responsibility, Jim Fay, Love & Logic Press

*Three Steps to a Strong Family, Teaching Your Children Values,
   Teaching Your Children Responsibility, Linda and Richard Eyre,
   Simon and Schuster

Habits of Goodness, Case Studies in the Social Curriculum, Ruth Sidney
   Charney, North East Foundation for Children

Facing Shame, Merele A. Fossum and Marilyn Mason, W.W. Norton
   and Co.

Struggling to Become a Role Model

Cheshbon Ha-Nefesh, Mendel of Santov, Feldheim Publishers

The Path of the Upright, Moshe Hayyim Luzzatto, Jason Aronson

On Repentance, The Thought and Oral Discourse of Rabbi Joseph Dov
   Soloveitchik, Pinchas H. Peli, Aronson

*Available from www.torahaura.com

SHMIRAT HA-LASHON— TEACHER CONFIDENTIALITY

Hevruta Study

That words are powerful may seem obvious, but the fact is that most of us, most of the time, use them lightly. We choose our clothes more carefully than we choose our words, though what we say *about* and *to* others can define them indelibly. That is why ethical speech—speaking fairly of others, honestly about ourselves, and carefully to everyone—is so important. If we keep the power of words in the foreground of our consciousness, we will handle them as carefully as we would a loaded gun.

Joseph Telushkin, *Words that Hurt—Words that Heal: How to Choose Words Wisely and Well*, William Morrow and Company, Inc., New York, 1996, pp. 4–5

Rabban Shimon ben Gamaliel said to his servant Tabbai, "Go to the market and buy me some good food." The servant went and brought back a tongue.

He told him, "Go out and bring me some bad food from the market." The servant went and brought back a tongue.

The rabbi said to him, "Why is it that when I said good food you bought me a tongue, and when I said bad food you also bought me a tongue?"

The servant replied, "It is a source of good and evil. When it is good, there is nothing better. When it is evil, there is nothing worse."

Leviticus Rabbah 33.1

Here are three short texts on *lashon ha-ra* (wounding with words).

Wounding with words is worse than wounding with swords because while swords do their damage from nearby, words can wound from a great distance.

Yerushalmi Peah 1.1

Wounding with words is worse than hitting a person. Hitting will affect the body, but words go much deeper. Bruises from a hit heal eventually. Wounds from words may never be healed.

Vilna Gaon

Someone told Rabbi Nahman: "If one puts a neighbor to shame in public, it is just like murder." Rabbi Nahman added on his own, "Why? When people are embarrassed their face turns first red—drawing blood—and then goes white as that blood is spilled."

Bava Metzia 58b

One who speaks *lashon ha-ra* always targets the faults of other people. A gossip is like a fly that always rests on the wound. If a person has boils, flies will ignore the rest of the body and hover over the sore. A gossip is just like them. A gossip ignores all the good in a person and speaks only of the evil.

Orhot Tzaddikim

Know that a person who agrees with a slanderous statement when he hears it is as bad as the one who says it, for everyone will say: "That person who listened to what has been said agreed with it, and that shows it must be true." Even if the hearer only turns to listen to the gossip and gives the impression of believing it…she helps spread the evil, brings disgrace on her neighbor, and encourages slanderers to carry their evil reports to all people.

Yonah ben Abraham Gerondi, Shaarey Tshuvah 3)

Just as a butcher is required to constantly study the laws of how to slaughter an animal in a kosher way, everyone is required to study the laws of *lashon ha-Ra*. When a person speaks he or she must always be aware of what one is allowed to say and what one is forbidden to say.

Chofetz Chayim

I have this thing that happens to me all the time. I will be visiting a synagogue and teaching some group (adults or kids). After a session I make a comment about some participant, like "That guy with glasses said some really interesting things," or "That girl seemed really angry." Then the professional with whom I am speaking starts to narrate. "That kid has three mothers and a sister with lupus. He is having trouble in school and is usually really difficult for us to handle. His comment to you was wonderful." I never say anything, but I am really conflicted about this information. On one hand, it is a lot more than I need to know. I feel I know too much about this kid, that I have been let into his family secrets. On the other hand, this is teacher gossip, and I love the three dimensionality it gives to the experience. The Chofetz Chayim, the leading expert in matters of the ethics of speech, speaks directly to this issue.

> The dedicated teacher often finds it necessary to discuss the progress and difficulties of students with parents, colleagues and principals. A lack of clear guidelines with regard to *lashon ha-ra* (improper speech) can create either a free-for-all atmosphere, where people talk about anyone with anyone, or, at the other extreme, a simplistic approach to *shmirat ha-lashon,* which could inhibit the teacher's effectiveness as an educator.

Simply put, teachers have lots of good reasons to share things about their students. In lots of contexts it becomes relevant to good educational practice. However, on other occasions, particularly because of the aloneness that teachers feel in the classroom, we often have a tendency to go beyond responsible professionalism and descend into gossip. Gossip is very much a moral issue that teachers must face. We know secrets about our students, secrets that we are often responsible for keeping.

> Generally speaking, the area of education and upbringing constitutes a constructive purpose which would permit relating negative information concerning a student. However, the specific conditions which permit speaking negatively for a constructive purpose must never be overlooked. Verification of facts is crucial. For a teacher to play amateur psychologist and hastily diagnose the student as having some complex disability or disorder without pursuing the matter properly constitutes recklessness–and the consequences can be devastating. To communicate one's evaluation under such circumstances would be *hotzat shem ra* (slander).

We often speak of this practice as labeling. We define a child as ADD or this or that syndrome and impose on him or her a name that will stick. While these behavioral patterns do exist and sometimes should be diagnosed and treated, when we teachers label a child with a behavioral pattern and lock him or her into that understanding, we are putting on the child a "bad name," and that violates Jewish law.

> It is an unfortunate fact that certain problematic children have not succeeded only as a result of having been misunderstood by a teacher, whose labeling tainted the image of that student in the eyes of all his/her future teachers.

We must be careful what we transmit to other teachers. There are some things that should be conveyed professionally to other teachers that will enable them to work successfully with a child they inherit. But think of the teacher conversation with phrases like "Oh, no, you're stuck with ____." It is a mitzvah to not reveal the secrets of others. Our students share many secrets with us, not so much by revealing them with words as by displaying them through actions. One of the responsibilities of good teaching is being trustworthy with our students' secrets.

> A teacher must make every effort to fully understand the behavior of each student; s/he must not be swift to condemn. It is essential that a student feel comfortable about expressing his/her true feelings to his/her teacher (in a respectable manner, of course). It is necessary to have a good heart-to-heart talk with the student before reporting a problem (unless one suspects that serious danger may be imminent).

There are times when we tell no one our impressions of our students, but still we label them. We lock in impressions of them, judge them once, and then hold on to that single image of how they will act and how they will perform. That, too, violates the Jewish value of "judging everyone favorably."

Teaching is about judgment. There are times to contact parents and times not to. There are times to report things to your principal and times to try to fix them on your own first. There are clear rules when things like suspected abuse or at-risk behavior must be reported, but things that are not of that scale can often be unclear.

A story: A high school student displayed out-of-control behavior. It was "a condition," not intentionally being difficult. My principal contacted the parents and said, "If the behavior does not change, the student will not be able to continue in the program." The student came back to school and blew up. He said, "You should have talked to me first. You didn't even give me a chance to change my behavior." I always felt he was right. We should have worked with him before we went to his parents.

> Finally, a teacher must be careful not to cause his/her student undue harm. At times punitive measures must be taken by the teacher for the maintenance of discipline

in the classroom or for the student's own development. Teachers must also bear in mind the long-term effects of relating or recording negative information about a student. The teacher must carefully evaluate just how necessary his/her actions are in light of their possible consequences.

Chofetz Chayim, A Lesson a Day, Day 60

We work hard to "control" our classrooms. Some students can fall victim to our hard work. As we "discipline" we can label; as we label we can bring shame. Teaching is an act of balancing many needs at once. Control is something we balance with respect, because we can manage our classroom and lose track of everything we have been trying to accomplish if we create harm, shame, or fear.

Speech and the Torah

Speech is mentioned lots of different times and ways in the Torah and even more in the Oral Torah (the Talmud, the Midrash, etc.). We are taught that God used words to create the world. That means that when we use words we, too, have the power to create or destroy. Here are just some of the categories of speech that Jewish tradition cites. Some of these should be avoided, some of them encouraged.

1. **RIKHILUT:** One who tells tales about another person breaks a Torah mitzvah: Do not go about as a talebearer among your people *(Leviticus 19:16)*. Who is guilty of *rikhilut*? One who goes from one person to another and says "So-and-so said this about Roger"; "I have heard such-and-such about Christine." Even if what is said or repeated is true, this telling of tales still ruins the world. *(Maimonides, Yad, "Laws of Ethical Conduct," 7.1-2)*

2. **LASHON HA-RA:** *Lashon ha-ra* is even worse. This means talking negatively about someone, even if what one says

143

is true. A person who speaks *lashon ha-ra* is one who says "Roger did such a thing," "Christine's ancestors were so-and-so," "I have heard this about Mr. Kline," and then proceeds to talk scandal...*(Maimonides, Yad, "Laws of Ethical Conduct," 7.2)*. One may speak truthful *lashon ha-ra* to "prevent physical, economic, or religious harm" to others *(Chofetz Chayim)*.

3. ***MOTZI SHEM RA:*** One who does *lashon ha-ra* by telling lies is a *motzi shem ra* (a slanderer) *(Maimonides, Yad, Laws of Ethical Conduct 7.2)*.

4. ***ONA'AT DIBBUR:*** *Ona'at dibbur* is the "speech crime" of saying things that cause others to feel shame or hurt. One good example of *ona'at dibbur* is using a nickname that reminds a person of something embarrassing. One famous example is asking a storekeeper the price of an object that you have no intention of buying. The understanding here is that by asking about it and then walking away you are leaving the store owner feeling bad about his merchandise or her pricing *(Bava Metziah 58b)*.

5. **SAYING "SHALOM":** It is a mitzvah to greet people. Psalms 34.15 says ASK FOR PEACE AND PURSUE IT. The interpretation of this verse is that it is a mitzvah to greet people we encounter *(Nedarim 8a)*. It is also an obligation to answer every greeting. The Talmud says "One who is greeted by another and does not return the greeting is considered to be a thief" *(Brakhot 6b)*.

6. ***TOKHEHAH:*** *Tokhehah* means "rebuke." Rebuke is telling someone that he or she is hurting him/herself, hurting others, or hurting you. It is a Torah mitzvah to provide *tokhehah*. The Torah says YOU MUST CERTAINLY GIVE *TOKHEHAH* (REBUKE) TO YOUR NEIGHBOR AND NOT CARRY A SIN BECAUSE OF HIM/HER. The Talmud extends this by saying that (a) you

should not give up on a person after only one try *(Arakhin 16b)*, but (b) one should not give tokhe*h*ah if it will be ignored or if it will make things worse *(Yevamot 65b)*. One of the interpretations of the last part of this verse, AND NOT CARRY A SIN BECAUSE OF THEM, is that tokhe*h*ah cannot be given in a way that publicly embarrasses or shames the one you are trying to help *(Maimonides, Laws of Character 6.7)*.

7. **RAKHOK ME'SHEKER**: *Rakhok me'sheker* means "keep far from lying." This mitzvah is based on Exodus 23.7, which says exactly that. Lying is against the Torah. However, the Rabbis create one kind of exception. "Rabbi Ilé taught in the name of Rabbi Eleazar son of Rabbi Simeon, "One can change the words of another in the interest of peace" *(Yevamot 65b)*. The most famous example of this is the permission to tell an ugly bride that she is beautiful *(Kethubot 17a)*.

8. **L'FNEI EVER**: *L'fnei Ever* means NOT BEFORE THE BLIND. In the Torah we are told YOU SHALL NOT PUT A STUMBLING BLOCK BEFORE THE BLIND *(Leviticus 19.14)*. In the Talmud *(Avodah Zarah 15)* we are told that a parent cannot strike an adult child because this might "trip" an adult child into hitting back. An adult hitting his/her parent is a capital offense. Likewise, saying anything that "pushes someone's buttons" and gets him or her to explode in anger is a violation of this principle.

9. **GOLEH SOD**: In the book of Proverbs it says ONE WHO REVEALS SECRETS IS A SLANDERER *(Proverbs 20:19)*. This verse created a mitzvah of not revealing or even seeking out other people's secrets *(Sha'arei T'shuvah 3.225, Sefer Halakhah 2.56)*. A *goleh sod* is a person who gives away other people's secrets. The Rabbis also taught that one should limit the telling of secrets, thus limiting the temptation to give them away. Reading someone else's mail is also a violation of "not seeking to know secrets."

10. ***TZ'NU'AT DIBBUR:*** In the midrash we are told that as
    God shaped each part of the first person God said to that
    part, "Be *tza'nuah"* (be modest). Sexuality is something
    designed to be a private part of relationships *(Genesis Rabbah
    18.3)*. The use of profanity and erotic speech is opposed to
    Israel's mission of holiness *(Deuteronomy 4.6, Shabbat 33a)*.

11. ***MILLEI TIKKUN:*** In his book *Words that Hurt, Words
    that Heal,* Joseph Telushkin defines a category, *millei tikkun,*
    words that heal. He learns four of these categories from
    our teacher Jack Reimer. Jack wrote a sermon called "Four
    Phrases to Live By." His four phrases were "Thank you,"
    "I love you," "How are you?" and "What do you need?"
    To these Rabbi Telushkin adds one more, "I am sorry."
    Judaism teaches that there are a large number of acts that
    one person should do for another. These include "healing
    those who are sick," "lifting up those who are depressed,"
    "teaching those who are ignorant," etc. Words are often
    the way we perform these obligations. The five phrases that
    Rabbi Telushkin teaches build relationships that heal and
    that maximize the image of God in each of us.

Teachers work with words. We may draw on the blackboard,
show media, dazzle with all kinds of other activities, but our
mainstay is words. Some of those words can hurt. Some of them
can heal. But most of all our words should enable growth and
self-actualization in our students.

Epilogue

Hebrew School Exile

Sam is a twelve-year-old who was arrested for selling Ritalin to friends at his private school as a recreational drug. Other parents in the Hebrew school have argued that Sam is a bad influence and should not be allowed to remain in Hebrew school. His parents tell Rabbi Shafer that a Torah education may be the one thing that can change Sam's messed-up values. Sam does not want to go to Hebrew school but will not become a bar mitzvah if he is removed from the school. He is not a pleasure to teach.

YOU BE THE JUDGE: *Should Sam be removed from the school to protect the other students?*

The Answer to "Hebrew School Exile"

1. It is a mitzvah to provide every Jewish child with a Jewish education. *Bava Batra 20b* makes it clear that starting just before 70 C.E., Joshua ben Gamala made it an obligation for every Jewish community to provide every Jewish student with a Jewish education—and it even sets limits on class size.

2. Even though we believe in universal education, Maimonides taught that one should teach Torah only to a student with good character. He suggests that one should first teach ethics to a student, and only when the student is ready to study Torah, teach the student Torah *(Laws of Talmud Torah 4.1)*.

3. In *Avot De Rabbi Natan* Bet Hillel argues that one should teach Torah to everyone because there were many sinners in Israel who were brought closer to God through Torah study *(9.9)*.

4. In *Midrash Shmu'el* it is explained that while Bet Hillel wanted to teach Torah to everyone, they did not necessarily want everyone in their classrooms. They were willing to teach everyone but wanted a fence between good students and unworthy ones *(Magen Avot)*.

5. *Bava Batra 20b* also makes a recommendation to place unmotivated students next to motivated students so that either (a) the motivation will rub off, or (b) the unmotivated students will not draw the motivated ones away from learning. Including everyone seemed to be important.

6. Rabbi Yehudah ha-Hasid *(Sefer ha-Hasidim, 189)* tells communal leaders, "It is better to throw out one bad one in order to improve the others who are good."

7. Still Rabbi Moshe Feinstein cautions, "If the student has a bad influence on others, certainly it is necessary to send him away. However, this judgment has to be made with great seriousness and much thought, because it is just like a decision of life and death."

The bottom line is this: If Sam learned from his experience and has done t'shuvah (repented and changed), then he should be allowed to attend class. If the school believes that he is teachable and that school is likely to be a good influence, he should be admitted. But if he is indeed a student who does not want to learn and threatens the teacher's ability to teach the rest of the class, the school is right in barring him from school—but should seek to find a private learning arrangement for him.

Here we are at the end of book. This last collection of sources gives us two truths. Teachers do have the power to remove students from their classrooms. But never forget what Rabbi Moshe Feinstein teaches: "As Jewish teachers we hold the power of Jewish life or of Jewish death." The future of the Jewish people is created, destroyed, or allowed to fall into neglect in your classroom.

APPENDIX

Here are explanations of the majority of the sources utilized in this volume.

Apocalypsis Mosis This a book that was not included in the Jewish Bible but was selected for the Apocrypha and Pseudepigrapha. It is a set of extra material about Adam and Eve.

Isaac ben Moses Arama (c. 1420–1494) was a Spanish rabbi and author. Upon the expulsion of the Jews in 1492 Arama settled in Naples, where he died in 1494. Rabbi Arama is the author of *Akedat Yitzhak* (*Binding of Isaac*), a commentary on the Torah.

Avot d' Rabbi Natan is sort of a coffee-table edition of *Pirkei Avot*. It is often included with copies of the Talmud (although it is not part of the Talmud) and contains sayings and maxims from various Rabbis from the mishnaic era.

Bava Batra is the third of three tractates of the Talmud that deal with damages.

Bava Metzia is the middle of three tractates in the Talmud that deal with damages.

Rabbi Yoshe Ber Rabbi Joseph Dov Ber (Yoshe Ber) was a relative of Rabbi Hayyim Volozhyner. In his youth he studied in the Volozhyn yeshiva and became renowned as a prodigy for his outstanding and keen intellect. It was said of him that as a child he already knew entire tractates by heart. As he grew into adulthood he became famous for his penetrating insight and incisive understanding of universal dilemmas.

Brakhot is the first tractate in the Talmud. Its central topic is prayers and blessings.

Martin Buber (1878–1965) was a Jewish philosopher, translator, and educator whose work centered on theistic ideals of religious consciousness, interpersonal relations, and community. Buber's major themes include the retelling of Hasidic tales, biblical commentary, and metaphysical dialogue. He is the autheor of *Tales of the Hasidim* and dozens of other books.

Yitzhak Buxbaum is a contemporary author specializing in the study of Jewish stories. Among his books is *Storytelling and Spirituality in Judaism.*

Chofetz Chayim "The Chofetz Chayim" is the nickname for Yisrael Meir Kagen (1838–1933). The name is taken from his major work, the book *Chofetz Chayim.* The book is about rules of ethical speech, particularly *lashon ha-ra.*

Rabbi Geoffrey W. Dennis Rabbi Dennis is a Reform rabbi. He currently teaches Jewish Studies courses at the University of North Texas and is the rabbi of Congregation Kol Ami in Flower Mound, Texas. His articles can be found in *Parabola, CCAR Journal,* and other publications.

Deuteronomy is the last book in the Torah, the first part of the Jewish Bible.

Deuteronomy Rabbah Deuteronomy Rabbah is an aggadic midrash on the Book of Deuteronomy.

Shimon ben Zemah Duran Shimon ben Zemah Duran (1361–1444), known as Rashbatz, was a Rabbinical authority and a student of philosophy, astronomy, mathematics, and especially medicine. Shimon was a very active literary worker. He wrote commentaries on several tractates of the Mishnah and the Talmud, while in his responsa he showed a profound acquaintance with the entirety of Jewish legal literature.

Ein Yaakov is a compilation of all the aggadic (legendary) material in the Talmud together with commentaries.

Encyclopedia Mythica Online encyclopedia on mythology, folklore, and legend.

Enoch Enoch is a book from the time of the Bible that did not make it into either the Jewish Bible or the Apocrypha that is part of the Catholic Bible.

Erhin A Talmudic tractate.

Eruvin A tractate of the Talmud that deals with "fences" that allow one to carry on the Sabbath.

Exodus is the second book in the Torah, the first part of the Jewish Bible.

Exodus Rabbah A midrashic collection on the book of Exodus. This is a late collection, probably edited in the 11th or 12th century.

Jim Fay is one of America's most sought-after presenters and authors in the area of parenting and school discipline. His background includes thirty-one years as a teacher and administrator, over two decades as a professional consultant, and many years as the parent of three children. He is the co-author of both *Teaching with Love and Logic* and *Parenting with Love and Logic* and dozens of other titles.

Rabbi Moshe Feinstein (1895–1986) was a Lithuanian rabbi and scholar who was world renowned for his expertise in Jewish law and was the *de facto* supreme rabbinic authority for Orthodox Jewry of North America. Feinstein's greatest renown stemmed from a lifetime of responding to religious questions posed by Jews in America and worldwide. He wrote thousands of responsa on a huge range of issues that affect Jewish practice in modern life. Among Rabbi Feinstein's works: *Igros Moshe* (Epistles of Moshe), a classic eight-volume work of legal responsa; *Dibros Moshe* (Moshe's Words), an eleven-volume work of Talmudic novellae; and *Darash Moshe* (Moshe Expounds), novellae on the Torah.

Rabbi Noson Tzvi Finkel, the Alter of Slabodka (1849–1927). His major work was *Or ha-Tzafun,* and he was the spiritual head of the Slabodka Yeshiva. Rabbi Finkel was one of the leaders of the Lithuanian Mussar movement.

Marc Gellman is the senior rabbi of Temple Beth Torah in Melville, New York. He is the author of *Does God Have a Big Toe?*, a collection of modern midrashim. With his friend Monsignor Thomas Hartman he published *Where Does God Live?* Gellman and Hartman host a cable television program called "The God Squad" and write a spiritual advice column syndicated in newspapers across the country.

Genesis The first book in the Torah and in the Bible. Genesis means "origins."

Genesis Rabbah (Bereshit Rabbah) is a midrash on the book of Genesis. It is traditionally attributed to the Rabbi Hoshaiah in the era of the Gemora.

Yonah ben Abraham Gerondi, also known as Rabbeinu Yonah and Yonah of Gerona (d. 1263), was a Catalan rabbi and moralist, cousin of Nahmonides. He is most famous for his ethical work *Shaarey T'shuvah, The Gates of Repentence.*

Haim G. Ginott (1922–1973) was a teacher, child psychologist, and psychotherapist who worked with children and parents. He pioneered techniques for conversing with children that are still being taught today. His book, *Between Parent and Child,* stayed on the best-seller list for over a year and is still popular today.

Rabbi Eliezer Gordon (1841–1910), also known as Reb Laizer Telzer, served as the rabbi and Rosh Yeshiva of Telz, Lithuania.

Haggigah is a volume of the Talmud that concerns Sukkot. *Haggigah* means "the holiday" in Aramaic, and Sukkot is considered to be "the holiday."

Havot Yair Rabbi Hayim Yair Bakhrakh of Germany (d. 1701) wrote this collection of responsa.

Hazon Ish Abraham Isaiah Karelitz (1878–1953) was known by his pen name, the Hazon Ish ("Vision of Man"). He was a rabbi born in Belarus who became leader of Haredi (super–Orthodox) Judaism in Israel. Karelitz devoted his life to the study of the Torah and Talmud as well as learning much science. He thought science was necessary for a full understanding of various aspects of Jewish law and practice. The true legacy of the *Hazon Ish* is the promotion of clarity in Talmud study, devotion in the worship of God, and loving-kindness in human interactions.

Samuel C. Heilman holds the Harold Proshansky Chair in Jewish Studies at the Graduate Center and is Distinguished Professor of Sociology at Queens College of the City University of New York. He is the author of a number of books, including *People of the Book.*

Hilkhot Deyot = The Laws of Belief. This is another section of Maimonides' *Mishneh Torah.*

Hilkhot Talmud Torah The section of Maimonides' *Mishneh Torah* that deals with rules of study.

Rabbi Samson Raphael Hirsch (1808–1888) was the intellectual founder of the *Torah im Derekh Eretz* school of contemporary Orthodox Judaism. He is the author of many important works, including *From the Wisdom of Mishle.*

Hoshea is a prophet who is found in The Prophets, the second third of the Hebrew Bible.

Rabbi Yitzhak Hunter, great Talmudist of the twentieth century, is the author of *Pahad Yitzhak* (The Fear of Isaac).

Isaiah is a prophet who is found in The Prophets, the second third of the Hebrew Bible.

Jeremiah is a prophet who is found in The Prophets, the second third of the Hebrew Bible.

Jerusalem Talmud There are two different collections of Rabbinic material known as the Talmud. The Jerusalem Talmud or *Talmud Yerushalmi*, often the *Yerushalmi* for short, and also known as the Palestinian Talmud, is a collection of Rabbinic notes. The other Talmud, often just "the Talmud," was written in Babylonia.

The Jewish Encyclopedia was an encyclopedia originally published between 1901 and 1906 by Funk and Wagnalls. It contained over 15,000 articles in twelve volumes on the history and then-current state of Judaism and the Jews as of 1901.

Rabbi A.Y. Kahn is the author of the *Tayyag Mitzvot.*

Keser Rosh or *Orhot Hayyim*, located in the back of some editions of *The Siddur HaGr"a* (The Gaon of Vilna) from Rabbi Hayyim Volozhiner.

Ketubot is a Talmudic tractate that deals with wedding contracts.

Hazrat Inayat Khan was a Sufi teacher from India who started the Sufi Order in the West (now called the Sufi Order International) in the early part of the 20th century. Though his family background was

Muslim, he was also steeped in the Sufi notion that all religions have their value and place in human evolution.

Lawrence Kohlberg (1927–1987) was an American psychologist. He served as a professor at the University of Chicago as well as at Harvard University. He is famous for his work in moral education, reasoning, and development.

Rav Abraham Isaac Kook (1864–1935) was the first Ashkenazi Chief Rabbi of Israel, the founder of the Yeshivah Merkaz ha-Rav, and a renowned Torah scholar. He was also both a mystic and a vegetarian. *Igorot HaRaiyah* are the collected letters of Rav Kook.

Lamentations Rabbah The midrash on Lamentations belongs to the oldest works of midrashic literature.

Laws of Character A section of Maimonides' *Mishnah Torah*.

Laws of Repentance Laws of Repentance is a section of Maimonides' *Mishneh Torah*.

Laws of Talmud Torah A section of the *Mishneh Torah* that deals with Torah study.

Leviticus, the third book in the Torah, the first part of the Hebrew Bible.

Leviticus Rabbah Leviticus Rabbah, *Vayikrah Rabbah*, is a homiletic midrash on Leviticus. It is was created somewhere between the 5th and 7th centuries.

Rabbi Yisrael Yaakov Lubchanski (d. 1941) was incarcerated in one of the ghettos during World War II. Despite the grim circumstances, Lubchanski's face constantly shone with joy. When asked how he achieved this state, he replied, "I exert myself to remove any signs of fear so I should not cause anyone else to become afraid."

Maimonides Rambam, Rabbi Moshe ben Maimon (Maimonides), 1135–1204. Spanish doctor, philosopher, and legal scholar. Born in Córdova, Spain, he moved to Morocco and finally to Egypt. Included in his works are the *Mishneh Torah*, a legal work that codifies all of the laws found throughout the Talmud; *Sefer HaMitzvot*, which lists and explains the 613 commandments; and the *Moreh Nevuhim*, a philosophical treatise.

Marganita Tava is by Rabbi Eliyahu Eliezer Silverstone of Southport, England (pub. 1956).

Meiri Rabbi Menachem Meiri (1249–c.1310) was a famous Talmudic and legal scholar. His commentary, the *Beit Ha-Behirah* (the chosen building), is one of the most monumental works written on the Talmud. This work is less a commentary and more a digest of all of the comments in the Talmud. His commentary was largely unknown for centuries until it was republished in modern times.

Meor Ha-Tokhehah A mussar book written by Rabbi Meir Kaplan (Jerusalem, 1951).

Michtav MaiEliyahu is by Rabbi Eliyahu Dessler (1892–1953). He is best known as the spiritual counselor of the Poneyezh yeshiva in Israel. He was one of the great modern Jewish thinkers. He was part of the Musar movement (concerned with character perfection and ethics) but was grounded in Kabbalah and Hasidism. *Michtav MaiEliyahu* has been partially translated as *Strive for Truth* (the first two Hebrew volumes of five have been translated into six English volumes).

Midrash Midrash is a body of literature that explicates the Biblical text.

Midrash Pinhas is a text created by Pinhas of Koretz, a disciple of the Baal Shem Tov.

Minhat Shmuel Rabbi Shmuel Weiss (c. 1890), a Hasidic rabbi, a descendant of the Maggid (Preacher) of Mezritch, wrote a work of responsa literature called *Minhat Shmuel* (on the fourth part of the *Shulkhan Arukh*) and also *Divrei Shmuel* (insights into the Talmud).

Mitzvot ha-Shalom A book of Mussar written by R. Yoseph D. Epstein (published in NY in 1969).

Thomas Moore is a psychotherapist, writer, and lecturer. He has published many articles in the areas of archetypal and Jungian psychology, mythology, and the arts. His books include *The Planets Within, Rituals of the Imagination, Dark Eros, Care of Soul, Soul Mates* and *Meditations*. He also edited *A Blue Fire* (HarperCollins), an anthology of the writings of James Hillman. Moore lived as a monk in a Catholic religious order for twelve years.

Rabbi Nachman of Bretzlav (1772–1810) Rabbi Nachman was a
Hasidic rabbi, the great-grandson of the Baal Shem Tov (the founder
of Hasidism). He emphasized living life with joy and happiness.
One of his best-known sayings is "It is a great mitzvah to be
happy." His main work is *Likutey Moharan*. Rabbi Nachman wrote
thirteen "Tales"—mythical stories of kings and wizards based upon
Kabbalistic thought. Rabbi Nachman died of tuberculosis at the age
of thirty-eight.

Louis I. Newman His *The Hasidic Anthology* is a collection of Hasidic
tales.

Orhot Tzadikim An anonymous mussar classic from the 15th century.

Rabbi Noach Orlowek An expert on child rearing, Rabbi Orlowek is
the author of *My Child, My Disciple* and *My Disciple, My Child*. An
acclaimed educator and counselor, he is presently *mashgiach* in
Yeshivas Torah Ohr in Jerusalem.

Peah A Talmudic tractate that has a central topic of leaving the corners
of fields for widows, the poor, and orphans.

Pele Yoat, Rav Eliezer Papo (1785–1826) wrote this classic mussar text
(with a Kabbalisitic underpinning).

Pirkei Avot is a minor Talmudic tractate that is sort of the Hall of Fame
of Rabbis of the Mishneh. It contains famous quotations and puts the
major teachers in context.

Rabbi Zelig Pliskin has devoted his life to helping people help
themselves. From his popular lectures at Aish Hatorah to his
innumerable counseling sessions to his wide selection of books,
Rabbi Pliskin is involved in providing proper tools to countless
people.

Proverbs is a book in the Writings section of the Jewish Bible.
According to a historical memory, King Solomon wrote it.

Psalms is a collection of 150 liturgical poems that is found in The
Writings, the third section of the Jewish Bible.

Rabbi Rafael of Bershid (d. 1815/6). A Hasidic master who was a
disciple of Pinhas of Koretz. He was well known for his honesty.

Ralbag Levi ben Gershon, better known as Gersonides or the Ralbag (1288–1344), was a famous rabbi, philosopher, and Talmudist. He is the author of *Ha'Deyot v'ha Midot.*

Rambam Rabbi Moshe ben Maimon (Maimonides), 1135–1204. Spanish doctor, philosopher, and legal scholar. Born in Córdova, Spain, he moved to Morocco and finally to Egypt. Included in his works are the *Mishneh Torah*, a legal work that codifies all of the laws found throughout the Talmud; *Sefer HaMitzvot*, which lists and explains the 613 commandments; and the *Moreh Nevuhim,* a philosophical treatise.

Rashi Rabbi Shlomo Yitzhaki, 1040–1105. French biblical and Talmudic commentator. Rashi is *the* commentator on the Bible and on the Talmud. He received his early Talmudic training in his native Troyes, France, before traveling to Mainz and Worms (Germany) and returned to Troyes at the age of twenty-five as one of the leading Talmudists of his day. He taught and wrote while earning his livelihood as a wine merchant. Rashi spent most of his life on his Talmud commentary. Rashi gathered around him a number of key students and studied with them daily. His commentaries grew out of these regular study sessions, and they provide the foundation on which most other Jewish commentary is based. He marked the trail others follow through this material. His later years were marred by the excruciating suffering of the Jews during the First Crusade in 1096, when many important Jewish communities were destroyed.

Rabbi Moshe Rosenstein is the dean of Tomer Devorah Seminary and a noted lecturer.

Rabbi Seymour Rossel is a rabbi, the author of dozens of books, and a lecturer. One of his works is *Managing the Jewish Classroom.*

The Book of Ruth is the story of Ruth, Naomi, and Boaz. It is a love story that is set in the time of the Judges, but it is found in the third part of the Bible, the Writings.

Rabbi Yisrael Salanter, 1810–1883. Israel Lipkin (known as Rabbi Israel Salanter, after his place of residence, Salaty) was the founder of the Mussar movement. Lipkin insisted on the practical application of the moral teachings of Judaism. He established societies for the study of religious ethics.

Samuel A priest and prophet who anointed both David and Saul as kings of Israel. His two books are found in the Prophets, the middle section of the Jewish Bible.

Sanhedrin is a tractate of the Talmud that deals with laws of courts.

Peninnah Schram has been called the doyenne of Jewish storytellers. Over the last two decades she has been crucial in creating a network of Jewish storytellers throughout North America. Peninnah is the author of many collections of Jewish stories.

Sefer ha-Midot leha-Meiri Meiri is Rabbi Menahem ben Solomon ha-Meiri (1249–1315). The Meiri was a thirteenth-century French scholar who devoted some eleven years of his life to compiling the *Bet ha-Behirah*, which is a staple for serious Talmud students. In the great controversy that raged in Provence during this period Meiri defended the study of philosophy and the sciences but stipulated that this study should be delayed until one has mastered the Talmud. He maintained an active halakhic correspondence with Rashba.

Shammai (50 B.C.E.–30 C.E.) was a first-century rabbi. He and Hillel were rivals, and their dialogue had a lot to do with shaping the Mishnah.

The *Shulhan Arukh* (literally: "set table") is a code of Jewish law composed by Rabbi Joseph Caro in the 1500s. It, together with its commentaries, is considered by the vast majority of Orthodox Jews to be the most authoritative compilation of *halakha* since the Talmud.

Lee S. Shulman is an educational psychologyst who has made notable contributions to the study of teacher education and the assessment of teaching. He is a professor emeritus at Stanford University.

Sifra is a legal midrash to Leviticus.

Sifrei refers to either of two works of midrash or classical Jewish legal biblical commentary based on the biblical books of Numbers and Deuteronomy.

Rabbi Joseph Soloveitchik The Rav, Rabbi Joseph Ber (Yosef Dov, Yoshe Ber) Soloveitchik (1903–1993), was an a leading American Orthodox rabbi, legal decisor, and Tamudist. He was also an existential Jewish philopher. He advocated a synthesis between Torah scholarship and Western secular scholarship as well as positive involvement with the broader community. He was the heir to the scholarship of Brisk, an important rabbinic family. Among his publications are *The Halachic Man* and *The Lonely Man of Faith*.

Sparks of Mussar Chaim Ephraim Zaitchik wrote *Sparks of Mussar*, a collection of short teachings and stories from great mussar (ethical) teachers.

Sridei Aish is a collection of responsa by Rabbi Yechiel Weinberg (1878–1966). He was born in Lithuania, where he became renowned as a Talmudist and the rector of the Hildesheimer Rabbinical Seminary.

Carol Starin was the assistant executive vice president of the Jewish Federation of Greater Seattle and director of the Jewish Education Council. She is the author of *Let Me Count the Ways I & II*, which offer five innovations for the Jewish classroom in the *Torah Aura Bulletin Board* and in two volumes.

Sukkah A tractate of the Talmud whose central topic is Sukkot.

T'nuat ha-Mussar This is a book on mussar by Rabbi Dov Katz, published in 1952.

T'shuvot Rav Akiva Eiger Rabbi Akiva Eger or Eiger (1761–1837) was a Talmudic scholar and influential legal decisor. This book is a collection of his rResponsa, his legal decisions.

Ta'anit is a tractate of the Talmud that deals with fasts.

Talmud The Talmud is a commentary and application of the Torah to fit into the modern life of the Greco-Roman era. It was created in two layers: the Mishnah (160 B.C.E.–210 C.E.) and the Gemora (200–500 C.E.).

Talmud Bavli *Talmud Bavli* is the Babylonian Talmud. The Babylonian Talmud is the product of taking the Mishnah that was created in the Land of Israel and adding a layer of commentary created in Babylonia between 210 and 500 C.E.

Tanhuma or Midrash Tanhuma is a midrashic collection that claims to be made up of the teachings of Rabbi Tanhuma. This is an older midrashic collection that was probably edited in the 5th century C.E.

Tanya (a.k.a. *Likkutei Amarim*, "collection of statements") is an early work of Hasidic Judaism written by Rabbi Shneur Zalman of Liadi, the founder of Lubavitch (Chabad) Hasidism, in 1797 C.E. The work is more commonly known by its opening word, *Tanya* ("it was taught in a *baraita*"). The work is both Kabbalistic and spiritual.

Rabbi Joseph Telushkin Joseph Telushkin (b. 1948) is a rabbi, lecturer, and author. Telushkin serves as a rabbi for the Synagogue for the Performing Arts and is an associate of the National Jewish Center for Learning and Leadership. Among his works is *Words that Hurt— Words that Heal*.

Tobit *Tobit* is a book that the Rabbis decided not to include in the Jewish Bible, but it was included in the Catholic Bible as part of the Apocrypha.

Torah Aura Bulletin Board Torah Aura is the publisher of this book. They produce a regular electronic newsletter for teachers. You can sign up for it by sending an e-mail to misrad@torahaura.com.

TorahQuest, a website devoted to Torah learning (**http://www. torahquest.org**) devolped by the Reconstructionist Education Department.

Vilna Gaon Elijah ben Shlomo Zalman (1720–1779) was a rabbi, Talmud scholar, and Kabbalist. He was also known as the *Gra* (a Hebrew acronym of Gaon Rabbi Eliyahu).The Vilna Gaon was a major opponent of Hasidism.

Rabbi Hayyim of Volozhin Rabbi Hayyim Volozhin or Reb Hayyim of Volozhin (1749–1821) was a Talmudist and ethicist. One of the most prominent disciples of the Vilna Gaon, Reb Chaim Volozhiner established the Volozhin Yeshiva. His major work is known as the *Nefesh ha-Hayim*.

Ron Wolfson is a faculty member of American Jewish University, a staff member of both Synagogue 3000 and The Consortium for the Jewish Family, and the author of the *Art of Jewish Living* series, *The Spirituality of Welcoming,* and *God's Top Ten List.*

Yad *is* the Hebrew word for hand. It is also equal to the number fourteen.

Yehil ben Yekutiel The Roman scribe Yehiel ben Yekutiel was the first to select specific virtues to guide Jewish behavior and action; he gave his thirteenth-century work, *Sefer Maalot ha-Middot,* authoritative muscle by citing biblical, Talmudic, and post-Talmudic Sephardic proof texts.

Rabbi Yehudah ha-Hasid (Judah the Pious), Judah ben Samuel of Regensburg (12th–13th centuries), the initiator of the German Hasidic movement. He was the author of *Sefer ha-Hasidim.*

Rabbi Yeruchem Levovitz (1875–1936) was an influential mussar teacher. Rabbi Levovitz first became *Mashgiach* (spiritual mentor) in the Mirrer Yeshivah in 1908, but during the dislocations caused by World War I he assumed various positions in different yeshivot until 1923, when he returned to his position in Mir. A collection of his essays is called *Da'at Hokhmah u'Mussar.*

Yevamot A Talmudic tractate that centers on discussions of the laws of levirite marriage.

Yoma is a tractate of the Talmud that deals with the laws of Yom Kippur.

Rabbi Yonah Rambam's cousin, Rabbi Yonah was the author of works on mussar such as the *Sharei Teshuvah, Sefer Ha-Yirah,* and many others.

Yoreh De'ah is a section of Rabbi Jacob ben Asher's compilation of Jewish law, *Arbah Turim.* This section treats all aspects of Jewish law not connected to the Jewish calendar: finance, torts, marriage, divorce, and sexual conduct. *Yoreh De'ah* is therefore the most diversified area of Jewish law. Later Rabbi Joseph Caro modeled the framework of his own compilation of practical Jewish law, the

Shulḥan Arukh, after the *Arba'ah Turim*. Many later commentators used this framework as well.

Zevaḥim is a tractate of the Talmud that deals with Temple sacrifices.

Rabbi Simḥa Zissel Ziv (1828–1898). He was a student of Rabbi Israel Salanter, the founder of the Mussar movement. Rabbi Ziv was the founder of the Yeshiva of Kelm.

The *Zohar*, the Book of Splendor, is one of the central books of the Kabbalah, Jewish mysticism. It is a midrashic commentary on the Torah written in medieval Aramaic and Hebrew. The work claims to be written by Rabbi Shimon bar Yoḥi but was probably written in the 1400s by a Spanish mystic, Moses de Leon.